Yarns of a Traveller

Yarns of a Traveller

Cliff Peel

First published in 2020

Your Biography

Published in Australia by
Your Biography
East Malvern Victoria 3145
yourbiography@optusnet.com.au
www.yourbiography.com.au

Typesetting and design by Bookpod

Front cover image: Road to Callemondah, Gnarwarre Road to the west, Gnarwarre, photo taken by Cliff Peel.

Back cover image: Twin engine steam train at Bacchus Marsh on route to Robinvale in Northern Victoria on the Ballarat line, photo taken by Cliff Peel.

Printed in Australia by IngramSpark

ISBN 978-0-6484300-2-5

A catalogue record for this book is available from the National Library of Australia

Further copies of this book, print and electronic, can be purchased through Your Biography, www.yourbiography.com.au, and Amazon, www.amazon.com.au/.

Contents

Acknowledgements

Thanks must go to my friends, some of whom I have named, who accompanied me on my adventures and in that way contributed unknowingly to many of these yarns. This book also reflects the care and professionalism of Gillian Ednie and Ev Beissbarth, the editorial and publication team from Your Biography, and the design and layout by Sylvie Blair of BookPOD. This team was also responsible for bringing my first book, *My Life in Broadcasting,* to life in 2016.

Last but definitely not least is the support and assistance I have had from my life partner, Rob Young, whose sub-editing advice, and help with illustrations and other matters, has been invaluable.

Why?

Since I was old enough to realise there was something different outside the house, I have had the urge to have a look at what was beyond the hill and the horizon. This has led me over the last eighty years to wonder what was around the next corner, across the river and at the end of the line. As a result I have visited sixty-seven countries and all seven continents.

On these travels I have met many interesting people, fallen in and out of love, seen some magnificent sights, and experienced some of the worst conditions in which many unlucky people are forced to live. I will not be telling you about the breathtaking natural scenery or the man-made magnificent edifices; they are there for you to see. Using an Australian term, I will be telling you yarns, or stories, about the interesting people and events that have happened to me while on the move.

The best way to describe my curiosity about what's around the corner is this first yarn. In my early teenage years my father drove, on several occasions, along the Princes Highway west of Geelong. Between Colac and Camperdown there were some stony hills known locally as the 'Stoney Rises'. A gravel road that wound its way from the highway through these hills disappeared in the distance. I was always intrigued as to where this little road would end. Years later, when I was able to drive, I travelled along this road to satisfy my curiosity. There was no dramatic vista at the end of it, just a farm gate leading to a house. However my curiosity was satisfied – I knew what was at the end of the road.

ONE

In the Beginning

I was born in 1936, so by the time I was old enough to appreciate travel World War II was in full swing. Travel was limited and petrol even more so. At the time the Peel family owned a holiday house in Lorne, 'Nardoo' in Smith Street and my first memories were travelling with my sister, Lynnette, from our farm in Gnarwarre, 20 kilometres west of Geelong, to Lorne in the back of a 1936 Ford utility. The speed limit for the country was 35 mph (60 km/h) for safety and to save petrol. New tyres were not available and worn tyres were retreaded time and again, and petrol was rationed. Hence the speed limit to save petrol and prevent tyres falling apart. The journey was along back roads through Winchelsea, Deans Marsh and Benwerrin. The road was gravel, and twisted and turned its way through the Otway Ranges with sharp corners and hairpin bends. Needless to say, there was very little traffic to worry about.

Once or twice we used the Great Ocean Road, taking a break at Anglesea and hoping we would not catch up with a convoy of Trans Otway buses. Four to six of these buses would meet trains at Geelong railway station and take holiday makers to Lorne. There was no way of passing these buses between Anglesea and

Lorne. They were always filled with passengers and were forced to use bottom gear going up the steep inclines because of the low-powered engines of the 1940s. During and immediately after the war, very few people in the city owned cars.

During the war years there was another trip that is etched on my memory. I think I was four or five, which makes it around 1942. We had to go to Melbourne for what I think could have been the funeral of my maternal grandmother. My father first had to get a permit to travel by road between Geelong and Melbourne. He also managed to get enough petrol-ration coupons to buy the fuel for the journey. He told me these details about the trip later when I was much older. He said that when he got the permit, he was told he must not stop on the road because at the time there were Air Force bases at Werribee, Point Cook and Laverton. If he had to stop, he had to display a white flag on the utility (still the 1936 Ford). He was also warned to ignore any aeroplanes using the utility for target location practice. I remember sitting in the front seat of the utility when between Werribee and Laverton a Winjeel training aircraft dived at our utility. I watched fascinated and a bit frightened as I saw this plane approach the utility, coming what I thought was very close to us and disappearing above us. Dad drove steadily on at the legal 35 mph. Whether he was unperturbed or not I will never know, but I still remember the plane approaching. The trainee pilot probably thought he had a good day, as there was a vehicle on the road for practicing finding a target.

A couple of times during the war my mother took me by train to Melbourne to visit her family. I was slightly overawed by the snorting black steam engine at the head of the train of red wooden carriages waiting patiently at Geelong station. When it was time to depart the stationmaster walked along the platform ringing a loud hand bell and making sure all doors where shut. On one trip we travelled at night. Once inside the compartment we had to pull down the wooden shutters over the window to block out the inside light. Before leaving I was shown the steam engine and the big light on its front blacked out with only a thin beam of light going onto the track, one of the many wartime blackout precautions. Needless to say, it was a slow journey. It only ended after an electric train took us from the then Spencer Street station in the centre of Melbourne to suburban Surrey Hills. The suburban train at the time consisted of wooden carriages which were either a 'dog box' with swinging doors on each compartment and no centre aisle or the later type which had sliding doors and an aisle the full length of the carriage.

TWO

More Room to Move

In 1946 I became a boarder at The Geelong College which meant that travelling of the legal type was very limited, although an occasional foray out a side gate on my bicycle allowed me to explore the Geelong environs to a certain extent. In May 1952 there were school holidays and, with the blessings of our parents, a classmate, Barton Stott, and myself decided to take one-man tents and hitchhike around Tasmania. I think the decision to let us go was helped by a very good friend of my father, the Reverend Clifford Auldist, who was the Presbyterian minister at the time in Launceston. We sailed from Melbourne to Devonport on the MS *Narooma*, took the rail motor to Launceston and stayed with the good reverend and his family.

We then started hitchhiking east through Scottsdale and the old mining town of Derby, reaching St Helens for our first night out. There were very few cars in those days and it appeared most were being used by travelling salesmen. One used picking us up as an excuse to deviate from the main road and visit St Columba waterfall, which he wanted to see. The next day we hitched our way to the centre of the state and stayed overnight at the historic town of Ross. The few cars using the roads stopped and offered

Rail motor at Davenport railway station, May 1952

us lifts, with the exception of one that stopped for the driver to apologise because there was no room. There must have been mum, dad and at least five children in the car. The following day we arrived in Hobart where we stayed at a cheap guesthouse. We had a look around the place and managed to race a double-decker Hobart tram. It began when I got off the tram and realised I had left my wallet on the tram seat. The conductor saw the wallet and waved it to me as I sprinted down the street and beat the tram to the next stop. I was fit in those days and the trams weren't the fastest. I retrieved the wallet and thanked the conductor.

The old convict settlement of Port Arthur was our next target and here we had a real stroke of luck. Another travelling salesmen had a car and a day off and wanted to visit Port Arthur and was happy to have the company of two hitchhikers. Not only did we visit the penal colony but were taken to some old coal mines

Cliff with rucksack and signpost, May 1952

where the convicts were employed mining coal and living in small underground cells which we were able to visit. At one stage the coal mine caught fire and at the time there was still heat in the ground.

Returning to Hobart, we decided we didn't have time to reach the west coast and chose to head for the Great Western Tiers in the central high country. At the time the Hydro Electricity Commission of Tasmania was building dams to store water to produce hydroelectricity. After leaving the small town of Boswell, HEC trucks carrying materials for the dams stopped and picked us up. Sometimes we covered only a few miles as they sometimes used only parts of the main road. Because of the loads, they travelled at between 10 and 20 mph.

It was a slow but sure way of eventually reaching Miena at the southern end of Great Lake and one of the highest points. This time the terrain defeated us as we could not find a flat space to pitch our tents, and it was very cold. The chalet at Miena was open so we used our emergency £10 note to spend the night in the chalet. A warm bed and a good breakfast were appreciated.

That day ended our Tasmanian odyssey as we arrived in Devonport and boarded the MS *Taroona* for the return trip to Melbourne. On that trip I learnt about seasickness. Barton, whose father owned a yacht, was not affected or impressed. Crossing Bass Strait we headed straight into a fearsome northerly gale. The *Taroona* had an interesting way of dealing with high winds. The bow went up as it ran into a wave and tilted to the left, then as the bow went down the ship tilted to the right, a perfect corkscrew motion. Not ideal for novice sailors. We arrived the following morning some hours late and the captain explained that, at the height of the gale, although the ship was going 'full steam ahead' it was actually going backwards.

THREE

Life after School

At the end of 1953, I left The Geelong College and went to work on my father's farm at Gnarwarre. My mother loved travelling and wanted to visit some friends in Brisbane but Dad wasn't leaving the farm. This resulted in my first long train trip as Mum didn't want to travel alone. This meant taking a train to Melbourne and boarding the Spirit of Progress at Spencer Street station. In 1954 the Spirit of Progress was hauled by a steam engine with the famous streamlined outer covering. It took four hours to arrive in Albury. Due to the change in railway gauges we transferred to the New South Wales Riverina Express at eleven o'clock at night in near-freezing conditions to arrive in Sydney the following morning. From there we got the Brisbane Limited to Brisbane which was quite uneventful, The standard gauge line from New South Wales only went as far as South Brisbane in those days so that's where we ended our journey.

On being shown around Brisbane I admired a fast-moving Mount Gravatt tram which our friend paced in her car at 45 mph (70 km/h). The visit also included a tour of Southport and Surfers Paradise, which was just starting to be eyed by developers. At the time it was a very desolate place: a cyclone had passed over it a few months earlier and what are now high-rise buildings were then just flattened bushes and land covered by sand. We returned to Melbourne and this took four days of travelling, again in three trains on two rail gauges. I still cannot understand the reason why Brisbane got rid of a very good and efficient tramways system.

Brisbane tram, August 1954

Working on the farm restricted my travelling. Most of my travelling was on weekend or day bus trips organised by the Geelong Young Farmers Club or the Ceres Young Peoples' Club.

Early in 1954, the event that every traveller eagerly waits for, the eighteenth birthday, and time to get a driving licence. I was quite relaxed about this because at the age of fourteen my father told me to get into the driving seat of the Ford utility and see if my feet could reach the pedals. They could and so I started my first driving lesson. As soon as I proved I could drive around the farm without wrecking the utility, I was using it to take fodder to the livestock, rabbiting, and (yuk) picking up dead and injured sheep. This continued for the next four years including illegal trips to the local post office to pick up mail, and in one case driving into Geelong to deliver some farm produce with Dad's warning words as I left, 'Don't run into anyone'.

On 29 April 1954, I went along with Dad to the police station in Belmont, a suburb of Geelong, to get my licence. Dad knew the sergeant at Belmont – he regularly shot rabbits on our property. The day was one Geelong footballers love; an icy wind was blowing from the south west along with the horizontal rain. The four policemen were gathered around a roaring log fire. The sergeant gestured to a young constable, who looked only a few months older than me, and told him to see if Mr Peel could drive. I drove carefully around the block doing four left-hand turns, and the young constable assured the sergeant I could drive. The discussion about the availability of rabbits continued, I was handed my licence and now I had legal wheels. A few weeks later another young farmer I knew went to his local country police station to get his licence, and was handed one on the spot. The sergeant said he knew he could drive because he had been watching him drive around the village for the past three years. I have always felt driving should be a compulsory secondary school subject starting when the students are fourteen or fifteen.

By now the Ford utility had gone and my parents had a new car. With my licence my parents decided another vehicle was needed. I wanted a Ford Zephyr convertible. The son of the local Ford dealer had one and I was envious. A new vehicle did arrive, a Standard Vanguard utility, ideal for feeding livestock and picking up dead sheep. So much for dreams! However I decided it could be good for camping and travelling and had a light wooden canopy made that easily fitted over the tray section giving a weatherproof cover for camping out. A large tarpaulin then covered the canopy and extended about a metre further out, providing an ideal mobile tent.

The next year I had another interesting train trip, this time from Melbourne to Balranald in southern New South Wales. One of my former classmates, Don Purton, whose father owned a pharmacy in Balranald, suggested that I and two other friends spend a couple of weeks camping on the junction of the Murrumbidgee and Murray rivers near Balranald. This meant getting the train from Melbourne to Echuca via Bendigo. At Rochester I was joined by Bruce Lloyd, another old Geelong Collegian, who lived nearby. At Echuca we boarded a small rail motor that travelled to Balranald on a branch line that is now closed. Bruce and I were able to sit in the front of the train beside the driving cabin. This was real country travel. The line had been built many decades ago to bring wool and livestock to the markets. By then the line was not in the best of shape so the speed was sedate to say the least. Twice the little rail motor ground to a crawl as a mob of sheep were hooted off the line. Nearing Yanga Lake siding the only other passenger aboard, a lady, asked the driver to start sounding the hooter. After a couple of prolonged blasts, a cloud of dust could be seen in the distance as the husband came to meet the train and collect the missus.

The stay on the river bank was very enjoyable, camping out, shooting and fishing, although we were warned not to use our .22 rifles on wild pigs as they tended to get upset and you needed much heavier artillery to stop them. That advice was taken and the only casualty was a kangaroo that got within firing range. After the break in the bush the little rail motor rocked us back to Echuca and three other trains eventually got me home.

I was able to make use of the Vanguard utility as a travelling campsite when another young chap, Daryl Gugger, whose father owned a farm nearby at Ceres, persuaded our respective families that we should extend our agricultural knowledge by visiting the Royal Sydney Show in March 1956. So the Vanguard was loaded up with mattresses, tarpaulins and provisions. It was a wet March and we encountered a flooded Midland Highway north of Shepparton. We travelled east along the Murray River and headed north through Cooma to Canberra. Near Cooma we put wet road driving to the test navigating a cutting filled with mud washed from the walls. In Canberra our navigating skills were tested trying to find our way off the many roundabouts, several times going around again to take the right exit. After that, driving into Sydney wasn't so bad. Sydney had trams then so following the tram lines made navigation easier.

Darryl Gugger in the Vanguard utility set up for camping, March 1956

After visiting the show over several days, and a visit to the Blue Mountains, we returned home along the coast on the Princes Highway. In those days it was a two-lane 'highway' with occasional patches of gravel. The steep descent down the Bulli Pass to Wollongong was a challenge especially with big coal trucks with doubtful braking systems close to the back bumper bar. It wasn't helped by seeing the safety runoffs at corners, where the trucks that lost their brakes could run up a ramp to stop. South from Bega the road became basic. In the twenty-first century, high bridges span the Towamba and Wallagaraugh rivers. In 1956, the road wound its way down the steep riverbank, crossing the stream on a concrete culvert with the water trickling across. Following heavy rain the road was blocked. Camping in the back of the Vanguard worked well but it did have its hazards. At Marlo, south of Orbost, there was no camping ground so we picked a pleasant spot at the mouth of the Snowy River. After dark several million mosquitoes claimed their territory so we had quite a fight on our hands as the modern sprays weren't on the market at that time. We made it home all right, coping with Melbourne traffic for the first time but then there was a bit more room to move around.

One year on it was time for another adventure. I was still in contact with Bruce Lloyd and along with one of his neighbours and friend, Max Bennett, we decided to drive to Mount Kosciusko, the highest point in Australia. We commandeered Bruce's father's Land Rover, loaded it with camping gear and headed east along the Murray River to Corryong at the foot of the Snowy Mountain National Park. At the time the Snowy Hydro Electricity Scheme was being built and beyond Corryong the whole area was controlled by the Snowy Mountain Authority. To travel in the park you had to get a permit from the Authority (SMA). On reading the not-so-fine print, it basically said that any collision with any SMA vehicle or any other problem was your fault, otherwise you were welcome. Needless to say SMA vehicles, often driven by new arrivals from overseas, were given plenty of room where possible. From Corryong, what is now called the Alpine Way (in those days a narrow gravel road) took us to old Khancoban, now moved and rebuilt. From old Khancoban the track went down the Geehi Walls, a narrow very steep descent into Tom Groggin. From there the track turned east to then undeveloped ski grounds around Thredbo. The descent down the Geehi Walls was really meant to be used by one vehicle at a time. The Land Rover was in bottom gear and four-wheel drive to control it and halfway down we met a utility coming up, again in bottom gear. I doubt if we could have stopped and the utility wasn't going to stop. With a cliff face on one side and a sheer drop on the other, it was a tight squeeze as we passed safely.

Cars on the summit of Mount Kosciusko, March 1957

After an overnight stay at Jindabyne, we drove to Mount Kosciusko on narrow gravel roads to find the small parking spot on the top of the mountain nearly filled with cars bringing a gaggle of politicians to the top of Australia. In 1957 you could drive right to the peak. Nearby there was Mount Townshend and in case it was found to be higher than Mount Kosciusko we got to its peak as well. We saw there was a two-wheeled track from the road to the top of Mount Townshend. Bruce and Max invited me to drive and as I eased it down a very steep incline they got out and helped guide me down to a little creek before driving up a less steep slope to the summit. After admiring and photographing the view I drove back to the main track. On the way up the very steep slope to the Kosciusko Road my companions rode on the bumper bar on the front. After reaching the main road I asked them why they sat on the front bumper. They then explained that on the steep ascent they noticed the front wheels starting to lift

Track up Mount Townsend, March 1957

a little and decided the extra weight on the front would balance the weight of our gear in the back of the vehicle. But they didn't want to tell me the vehicle may have somersaulted until safely on a more even keel. One thing I learnt was what you don't know you don't worry about.

Because of the trip to Mount Townshend it was getting dark so we camped beside a small lake near the Chalet at Charlotte Pass, not far from the summit of Mount Kosciusko. It was cold with some snow still on the ground. Next morning in a show of bravado I went for a very swift and short dip in the lake. I can't remember if my two companions were silly enough to do the same.

Having reached our objective, we then planned to head for the most southerly part of mainland Australia, Wilsons Promontory. From Jindabyne we took a mountain track south past The Pilot, crossing the Indi River at the point where the state borders become a straight line to the coast after following the Murray River. Carefully weaving our way through the scrub we arrived at the border at a place called Quambat Flat, marked by the remains of a crashed aircraft and the Indi River. Without getting his feet wet Bruce was able to stand in two states with the stream flowing below him. Many years later when he was a politician I pointed out to him his ability to straddle both sides.

It was while we were in this remote part of the country with not a garage in sight the gasket on the petrol pump gave up. We kept the Land Rover going and kept the petrol flowing with the help of cardboard from a Weetbix box (thank you, Sanatarium). The cardboard gasket lasted about eighty miles before needing to be replaced. The first place we could get a proper replacement was in Sale in Gippsland. From there we made our way through South Gippsland to the Tidal River camping ground at Wilsons

Bruce Lloyd astride the Murray River, Quambat Flat, March 1957

Promontory. We spent a day hiking to the southern point of the Promontory and back to the camping ground along a very basic track which in places meant wading through water between thin, high saplings. The easiest part of the trip was the return drive to Bruce's home at Nanneella in Northern Victoria.

FOUR

From Country to City

A month after returning from the Snowy Mountains excursion I turned 21 and also changed the direction of my life. I left the farm and moved to Melbourne to attend the Vincent School of Broadcasting, planning to become involved in the radio industry, and even possibly the recently introduced field of television. The departure from Gnarwarre was on quite amicable terms which meant I was again able to borrow the Vanguard utility, complete with canopy, for another trip.

At the broadcasting school I had teamed up with a chap my age, Ian Williams, and in August 1958 we set off for a drive to southern Queensland. We decided it would be a good opportunity to have a look at outback Australia. We headed north to Mildura, across the Murray to Wentworth, then north to Broken Hill and the remote township of Wilcannia. We followed the Darling River to Bourke on a dirt track which when wet turned into impassable grey mud, but when dry was a hard concrete surface of corrugated grey earth. The weather was hot and halfway to Bourke was the little settlement of Louth which was supposed to have a hotel. There was no pub (it had burnt down earlier in the year) but the hotel was still selling beer from a makeshift shed. The beer was warm but still welcome.

Wilcannia–Burke Road, Louth, July 1958

We reached Bourke without too much obvious damage to the Vanguard's suspension. We made our way across northern New South Wales, then headed north to Goondiwindi in Queensland and onto Chinchilla on the Darling Downs. Ian was able to meet a friend of his from national service days so we spent a day there before enjoying the delights of the Gold Coast. There we exchanged the rigours of camping in the back of the Vanguard for the comforts of a recently built motel.

We returned to Melbourne along the coast. The first night out from the Gold Coast I remember well. We left Murwillumbah in northern New South Wales in pouring rain which got worse as the day wore on. By nightfall we could not find a place to camp and eventually, as it was too wet to even get the tarpaulin across the canopy, we sort of slept sitting up in the front of the utility. At daybreak it was dry enough to get out and stretch our legs. We drove on over the next few days through Newcastle, Sydney, the south coast of New South Wales and eventually Melbourne in Victoria. The Princes Highway between Sydney and Orbost had not improved since I last travelled on it. The low culverts were still in place. At Orbost we were better prepared for the mosquitoes as once again we camped by the Snowy River.

FIVE

New Horizons

The following year, 1959, was the year my horizons were expanded. In April my career in radio and television began with the Vincent School of Broadcasting recommending that I accept a job as a copywriter-announcer at 2QN Deniliquin in southern New South Wales. So I farewelled my clerical job at the Crown Law Department, my night school, and my parents still on the farm at Gnarwarre. I was wondering how I was going to get to Deniliquin, not having a car while at night school in Melbourne. Dad solved the problem by presenting me with a ten-year-old Vanguard Estate car, the English version of a station wagon.

I now had wheels and also another vehicle that I could use for camping trips, as it had back doors and the back passenger seat folded forward giving me room for mattress or sleeping bag. In the 16 months I was at Deniliquin, I used it to drive around the area, the Southern Riverina as it is called, including one of my favourite spots, the Barmah Forest on the banks of the Murray River. The age of the Vanguard showed up in one trip when my landlady wanted to see a polo tournament at Wakool, an hour's drive from Deniliquin. The road was gravel, dusty and corrugated. The Vanguard was parked amongst the Rovers, Mercedes and other classy cars that polo players drive. My landlady watched the polo from the grandstand while I, with screwdriver in hand, tightened the door and other screws that had worked their way loose on the way. The performance was repeated after the return trip. The same operation was needed after a friend and I drove to Hillston on the Murrumbidgee to watch the annual rodeo.

I finally farewelled the Vanguard after reporting on a fire at a sawmill at Mathoura between Echuca and Deniliquin. I had got an interview on tape with the owner of the mill and was pushing the Vanguard to its limit to get back in time for our local news service. The 70 mph (110 km/h) I was doing was too much for the poor old car, and the engine gave up the ghost – a valve dropped through the cylinder, I was later told. By luck, right behind me was one of the lads from the town who stopped and towed me back in his very powerful early 1950s Chevrolet, faster than the Vanguard could have managed. Being towed at that speed is not a pastime I would recommend. We made it in time for the news service unharmed.

The next day the Vanguard was pushed to the local Standard dealer where it was traded in for a Triumph Herald sedan which had recently arrived from England. This was a sturdy little car and was registered with New South Wales number plates so I had to get a New South Wales driving licence although I was able to retain my Victorian one, which I kept up to date no matter where I was.

My next move was to local radio station 4VL in Charleville in south-west Queensland where I was offered slightly more pay and the opportunity to establish a local radio news service. I drove there through Armidale in northern New South Wales and cut across to Derby in southern Queensland before heading west.

The next main town was Roma and after that the bitumen road turned into a corrugated gravel road where crossing creeks and waterways meant going down the bank, crossing on a concrete slab and climbing out again. Five hundred miles from Roma I arrived in Charleville. The first bitumen I travelled on was when I turned into the main street.

The Triumph Herald, despite the rigours, was in very good condition. The local dealer was amazed that the small car made it and the local apprentices enjoyed working on the car as they could practically pull it apart and put it together again. I also had to get it registered in Queensland and also get a Queensland driving licence. At the police station I showed the sergeant my other driving licences but he said, 'This may sound ridiculous considering where you have driven from, but I still have to see if you can drive.' We drove around the block and I got what turned out to be a most valuable piece of paper. The licence was for ten years' duration but the problem was that it was on a piece of paper that quite often couldn't last that long. I have seen some licences that were covered in sticky tape just to keep the paper together. Sometime later when I was in strife in Victoria getting myself confused or going the wrong way, all was generally forgiven by the local constabulary when I produced the Queensland licence issued in Charleville and in a broad outback Australian accent explained I didn't often drive in the big city.

In the 15 months I was in Charleville I took the opportunity to visit many of the local waterholes and scrub but very rarely travelling at night because of the kangaroos. They have a bad habit of jumping into car headlights. The skies were generally clear at night so I travelled with only the sidelights on unless another car was coming towards me. If driven by a local, the car would flash its headlights and revert to its sidelights. I had a first-hand experience with the problems of kangaroos when three new-found friends suggested we go to Morven for a dance some 50 miles east of Charleville on what was laughingly called the Warrego Highway – the road that I originally drove to Charleville on. Because of the nature of the road I had to use headlights. On the way back I saw the first kangaroo in time to swerve, and it hit the car and somersaulted over the front of the bonnet. The next one I spotted hit the rear of the car and spun over the back. The third one I did not see and it jumped straight into the front passenger door. The kangaroo bounded off, no one was hurt but the door was badly dented and the front-seat passenger had to leave the car through the driver's side. Next day the local garage apprentices had a great time straightening out the dents and getting the car roadworthy again. They did a very good job.

The problems for travellers caused by kangaroos was demonstrated to me one night when I was at the Charleville airport. I was talking to the Royal Flying Doctor Service officer when he said, 'Come outside and watch the Flying Doctor plane land.' I asked, 'What's so exciting about that?' and he answered, 'You'll see.' In the distance I could see the Dover plane approaching with its landing lights on. At the same time, a powerful truck with a large crash bar on its front drove up to the end of the runway, then turned around and came along the runway at full speed with its lights on and horn blaring as the Dover touched down and more or less tailgated the truck to the terminal. The RFDS officer said that with scrub up to the boundary of the airport it was the best way they knew of making sure kangaroos did not bound into the lights of the aircraft. He said the Flying Doctor pilots were used to it but commercial pilots who had to make an emergency landing found the experience quite traumatic.

The next move was in March 1961 when I applied for and got the job of assistant regional journalist at the ABC's Rockhampton office. Once again I challenged the Warrego Highway, leaving Charleville behind and arriving unscathed at Roma to meet the bitumen. In the 1960s the Queensland government was doing its best to put in all-weather roads in the outback to get livestock as quickly as possible to the coast for export. The locals called these roads 'crystal highways'. Because of the distances covered and the cost, these roads were just strips of bitumen one vehicle wide. When two vehicles passed in different directions, both had to have one set of wheels off the road in the gravel, throwing up showers of stones that often shattered windscreens. One trick I learnt very quickly was when a truck or fast car was approaching was to get

Triumph Herald convertible, Emu Park, August 1961

right off the bitumen and signal the other driver to stay on the hard surface. I am certain that action saved me a few windscreens.

The trip to Rockhampton was via Brisbane where I spent several days being shown how the ABC news gathering system worked at the state headquarters. Then the Triumph Herald took me safely in one day from Brisbane to Rockhampton, a long day's drive of 600 miles (965 kilometres). Between my arrival in March and the following August, I spent a lot of my spare time driving around my new environs, including the seaside resorts of Yeppoon, Keppel Sands and Emu Park where I joined the Surf Lifesaving Club.

Early in August on the ABC morning news it was announced that Australian Motor Industries which assembled Triumph Herald cars in Australia had gone broke. I was in the office at the time and I received a phone call from the local Triumph dealer, asking if I was interested in a new car. I told him I had heard the news and he explained that he had several of these Australian-assembled Triumph Heralds in stock and suggesting that I could be interested in a trade-in. Due to the circumstances I can say the changeover price was very reasonable and so later that day I drove away with a fire-truck red Triumph Herald convertible and the dealer had a sturdy English assembled sedan for sale. It didn't take me long to work out why the local assembly company went broke. There was very little or no quality control on the product. There were a lot of problems that occurred that should not have happened with proper workmanship. On the positive side it was a great 'pick-up truck' with young males and females happy to be passengers. I did have a lot of fun with it. My favourite trick when stuck in a long line of traffic, like going to the beach at Emu Park at the weekend, was to drive standing up with one hand on the windscreen for balance and the other on the steering wheel, one foot on the floor and the other either on the accelerator or the brake pedal. I had to sit down to change gears (no automatic cars in those days).

In the remaining 18 months while I worked in Rockhampton, I did some long-distance trips in the convertible including a weekend at the Gold Coast for surf lifesaving championships. That meant driving to the Gold Coast after work on Friday, arriving early the next morning, and leaving Sunday afternoon to get back in time for work on Monday afternoon. On the return journey somewhere north of Bundaberg, I had one of those possibly fatal mini-naps, waking in time to avoid taking out a white guidepost on the wrong side of the road. Lesson learnt, I pulled over got out of the car, wrapped myself in a tarpaulin I had in the back, and slept for four hours on the ground beside the Bruce Highway. It's a lesson for all long-distance drivers.

The first time I drove the convertible to Melbourne resulted in a traffic jam at Surfers Paradise on the Gold Coast. My sister and her friend had come up to visit me and tour North Queensland and, as I had some leave, like a good brother I drove them back to Melbourne. We had a break at Surfers Paradise and my sister and her friend went one way for the day and I went the other. After booking into the motel I changed in to T-shirt, shorts and thongs. It was the first and last time I drove in thongs. Crossing the Nerang River, then a narrow two-lane bridge, the car in front stopped suddenly, my thong-clad foot got caught between the brake and the accelerator and I redecorated the car in front and the front of my car. The car I bumped into was not badly damaged and no one was hurt, but my car was immoveable with its front pushed against the wheels. Half an hour later the tow-truck turned up, delayed by traffic at a standstill on the Pacific Highway. As mentioned earlier, in those days there was only one lane each way. Once the convertible was loaded onto the truck normal traffic resumed. A miracle worker at the repair shop got the convertible going again, and I drove to Melbourne and back with a thick leather strap around the front bonnet to hold the whole thing together.

On returning to Rockhampton I was in urgent need of transport and ended up with a second-hand but reliable Holden car with a solid roof. Incidentally with the convertible, the driver and front passenger did not get wet if it rained if you drove fast enough. The back-seat passengers weren't so lucky. There was a canvas roof for use in wet weather.

In May 1963 my career continued on its upward trend and I received a promotion to move to the ABC office at Sale in Gippsland (eastern Victoria). The ABC wanted me in Sale as soon as possible and suggested I get a quote to send my car by rail. It changed its mind after I gave them the quote for the car to go through three different railway systems. Then it was suggested I send it by ship through the new Rockhampton port of Port Alma. That idea was not followed through after the shipping agent said that the car could sit there for six months before going anywhere if it hadn't rusted away in the salty atmosphere. The ABC, bless its heart, paid me to take five days to drive from Rockhampton to Sale.

I took the prescribed time to get there with only one incident when the still legal Charleville licence again helped me out of a spot of bother. I came down the Newell Highway to avoid the Pacific Highway and the several ferry crossings in northern New South Wales. On one remote section I checked my rear-vision mirror and pulled out to pass a slower car, unaware that there was a motorcycle policeman right on my tail and in the blind spot. A rather agitated constable pulled me up and gave me some stern words about not looking out for other vehicles. As requested, I pulled out my licence and explained matters in a good western Queensland drawl what had happened. As he was considering whether it was worthwhile trying to fine someone in a car with Queensland number plates, not to mention an address in the back of beyond, another motorcyclist sped past. He was moving much faster than even the Holden could do and this proved a much better challenge for the policeman who told me to be more careful and sped off in hot pursuit. I think I still have the now expired Queensland licence on its original paper.

On arriving in Sale I found some accommodation in a large flat in a rambling house. In my spare time I explored the surrounding countryside to again become more familiar with the area where I was now living. I was at Sale for 15 months and managed to see most of Gippsland which included one journey over the Australian Alps giving me a taste of the high country wilderness. This took me, along with a friend, from Sale to Mitta Mitta, camping in one of the log huts built for tourists and stockmen, to our destination of Albury. We returned much the same way. During the stay in Sale, the Holden was upgraded to a more recent second-hand Holden, being slightly more reliable for the Gippsland and Alpine roads.

Back to the Metropolis

In August 1964 the head of ABC Television News in Victoria visited Sale and asked if I was interested in working in the Melbourne newsroom. The answer, given in less than 30 seconds, was 'Yes!' At that point I had about six weeks of annual leave owing so I was told to take it and then start work on my new career in television.

While working in Rockhampton, the furthest north I had travelled was Mackay so this was a great opportunity to go further north to Cairns. This also gave me the opportunity to travel on the new Southern Aurora train that ran on the recently built standard gauge to Sydney. It was a first-class sleeper train designed for the business traveller as well as the tourist. It left both cities at eight o'clock each night arriving at its destination at nine o'clock each morning. There were dining and lounge cars available, allowing travellers to arrive fed, showered and shaved ready for work in the heart of the city. I used it for many years moving between Melbourne and Sydney.

On this trip I kept moving north travelling on the Brisbane Limited, the overnight train to South Brisbane. I learnt one trick on this train. Between Sydney and Grafton you could only get one drink with your meal, but the buffet crew changed at Grafton, and the new crew was much more easy going as you went further north. (It helped if you bought them a beer.) There was no lounge car on this train so the buffet area with seats at the bar was a good place to meet fellow travellers. From Brisbane, the Sunlander train with its mixture of sleeping and sitting apartments made its leisurely way over three days to Cairns. The narrow gauge track wound its way through hills and valleys stopping at large and small stations on the way. It was interesting to see the scenery gradually changing from sub-tropical to lush rain forests as you travelled north.

As every tourist does I took the train to Kuranda which winds its way beside the Barren River up to the top of the Great Diving Range. In 1964 the train was hauled by a steam engine. The rear carriage had a viewing platform – an ideal place to take photographs and also the ideal place to get covered in soot from the steam engine. By the time I returned to Cairns I could have auditioned for a black and white minstrel show.

The Cairns–Kuranda train on Stoney Falls rail bridge, Kuranda, August 1964

In Cairns I had a stroke of luck and met a young man who lived further north at Port Douglas. We were mutually attracted or, to be honest, it was a love affair, and so very soon I was being shown the beaches north of Cairns and the then very quiet village of Port Douglas, now a popular tourist resort. My new-found friend, Ron Cooper, had a small house on the hill overlooking the four-mile beach on Trinity Bay. At the time there were two hotels, the blue pub near the waterfront and the pink pub in the centre of the township. They both had actual names but the locals called them that because one was painted a light blue and the other pink. Ron was very keen to show me around so I was taken to places like the Mosman Gorge and even drove to Townsville south of Cairns and took the launch trip to Magnetic Island. I was also introduced to the Atherton Tableland which included Lake Barrine and the Tinaroo Falls Dam. All good things must come to an end, including holiday leave. After a fond goodbye to my friend and Northern Queensland I used my return tickets to get back to work in Melbourne. The tickets were an interesting series of tickets joined together, which covered various sections of the journey. As you passed through each section the conductor tore off the appropriate ticket, the last being from Albury to Melbourne.

I settled into my new career, outlined in my first book *My Life in Broadcasting*. By June 1965 my annual leave was due. In journalism at the time we received six weeks' leave because under our award we were expected to work at very odd times on any five of the seven days in a week without penalty payments. The lure of the north again attracted me and this time I made my destination Darwin.

The first leg was from Melbourne to Adelaide on the Overland train that ran overnight on the broad gauge line to Adelaide through Ballarat, Horsham, Serviceton and Murray Bridge.

There was a very steep climb from Bacchus Marsh just west of Melbourne up to Ballan on this side of Ballarat. Our new diesel locomotive found the climb hard work. In the days of steam an extra engine or engines were added at Bacchus Marsh and taken off at Ballan. On the trip to Melbourne the engines were also used as brakes on the downward journey especially for heavily laden wheat trains. From Adelaide a local broad gauge train took me to Port Pirie where I joined a standard gauge train to Maree. A new standard gauge line had just been built to bring coal from Leigh Creek near Maree to power stations in Port Augusta and for export. At Maree I joined the famous narrow gauge Ghan train. Up to a few years previously, the train started from Port Augusta and wound its way through the Pichi Richi pass to Quorn and Maree. Now it terminated at the end of new line at Maree. Then it followed the original route to Alice Springs. The present-day Ghan train travels on a completely different route on standard gauge track to Darwin. The Ghan I travelled on was made up of a variety of carriages passed on mainly from the old Trans Australian train, now replaced by the Indian Pacific train. The old Ghan had sleeping and sitting carriages, several lounges and for first-class passengers a very elegant dining car which came from an earlier era. At the front of the train there were trucks carrying cars and other vehicles. The road north from Port Augusta was then a gravel track.

The maximum speed for the Ghan then was 35 mph (60 km/h). The reason for this was that the track had been built literally on the ground. Weather records and communications weren't as reliable as they are now, which meant that if there had been a storm and part of the line had been washed away or a high wind had covered it with sand, the driver had to be able to stop the train within his line of sight. The Ghan took two days to travel to Alice Springs with the major stop at Oodnadatta. Here the train stopped for about half an hour and quite a number of the passengers took the opportunity to head for the local hotel a short distance from the station. We were told that once we heard the train's horn blowing we had five minutes to get back on board or wait another week for the next train. The threat was enough to make sure all were aboard at the right time.

At Alice Springs I had the opportunity to fly to Ayers Rock as it was then called. Uluru, the name used by the indigenous population, eventually became the accepted title. In those days it was not a great tourist destination. The rock is about 400 kilometres from Alice Springs and at the time there was only a gravel road to the site. A local airline, Connellan Airways, flew visitors there and had a lodge there with the only licensed bar. Our small two-engine plane took off from Connellan's original

The Ghan train at Oodnadatta, June 1966

airport within the town boundaries. There were three passengers and the pilot onboard with every inch of remaining space loaded with goods for the lodge. On the way the pilot asked if we would like to see Palm Valley, a gully with unique palms growing in it. We did a low flight over that and when we arrived at the Rock we did several passes over it so we could take photographs.

Then we came into land. To me the strip at the time looked to be about a cricket pitch in length with trees right up to the edge. I was in the co-pilot's seat and remember the plane – not only full but possibly overloaded – coming into land on this short dirt strip. The pilot had landed here before and seemed quite relaxed as we just about touched the top of the trees at the approach and then landed in a shower of dust with all brakes on and the engines in reverse, as another lot of trees appeared to be coming towards us at a great speed. Needless to say we stopped in time.

I climbed the rock and later watched the sun set. I stayed overnight and next day took the flight back to Alice Springs. The plane was again well loaded. Taking off we began as far back on the strip as possible and once the engines were at full throttle we took off, just clearing the trees at the end of the runway.

The next move north was by the Ansett Pioneer mail bus which took three days to cover the journey to Darwin. (The Ghan at that time stopped at Alice Springs.) There were 32 people aboard the bus who shared the front eight rows. The remainder of the bus and the four-wheeled trailer it was pulling was filled with mail bags. It was definitely the mail bus. The passengers who had travelled on this service before began taking bets about when the bus would break down, not if. It did, of course, within eyeshot of Newcastle Waters homestead, which was a bit reassuring for possibly stranded passengers. The driver was trained to cope with these incidents and, after disappearing under the bus for a while had it going again. A regular passenger told me the run was where the Ansett company pensioned off its old buses. At towns, settlements and mail boxes beside the Sturt Highway, the main road to Darwin, the bus stopped to deliver and collect mail. The bus also stopped at several roadside monuments where one enthusiastic passenger took photographs which included his young son standing on or beside each monument. The overnight stops were at Tennant Creek and Larrimah. Here the hotel couldn't accommodate all the passengers so some stayed at the local police station. The passengers and driver were a friendly mob and it was an interesting trip.

In Darwin I only had two days there before moving on. I wanted to go to Mount Isa and then return to Melbourne by train. There was no bus service so the two options were flying or hitchhiking. I considered the budget and so chose the cheap option of hitchhiking. On the first day I made it to Adelaide River from several lifts. At the hotel I ran into a young American tourist at dinner who was driving a Land Rover around Australia on his own. He was on his way to Mount Isa. Did he want someone to talk to on the trip and do some driving? Yes, he did, and that was a stroke of luck.

It was a two-day trip to Mount Isa and so we stopped at the Frewena roadhouse on the Barkly Highway halfway to our destination. The roadhouse was basic to say the least. One long shed with the rooms divided by hessian walls for visual but not sound privacy. We had dinner at the bar which served as a food counter as well as for drinks and then retired early to bed sharing one of the compartments. At about eleven at night a couple arrived from Tennant Creek and it turned out they had got married that day and Frewena was the nearest place they could stay for their first big night. All this became obvious as the couple got to know each other intimately. The bride was a bit hesitant at first but there was a happy ending. Then after a period of quiet newfound enthusiasm returned, with the bride by now more eager. By this time, I can guess, most guests were eagerly waiting for the next episode. As mentioned there was no sound proofing. That again had a happy ending. Some time later, the by now quite enthusiastic bride made another claim on the groom who, admitting defeat, said in a fairly loud whisper, 'Oh, not again.' The other guests were very restrained and only a few muffled titters could be heard. Next morning after going outside and laughing loudly we were at the bar having breakfast when the groom arrived looking the worse for wear. He was greeted by the landlady who asked him how things were going and then looked at him and said, 'You need a big glass of milk!' In the outback there are not too many choices for the location of the wedding night. On arriving in Mount Isa my American tourist said the night at Frewena was definitely something he could write home about as I thanked him for the lift.

Mount Isa revealed to me the extent of mining in Queensland but the town itself looked a fairly rugged and tough place to live. I still had time left in my leave to get the Inlander train which took me east to Townsville, then the Sunlander to Cairns. I had several days there catching up with my friend from the previous trip, Ron Cooper, and this included another drive to Port Douglas, where the décor of the blue and pink hotels had not changed. With leave time running out, the remaining six days was spent on three trains taking me from Cairns to Melbourne. My appetite for travel especially in the north of Australia was certainly being satisfied. Like all good things holidays had to be earnt, so there was another year to wait before being able to head off into the unknown.

SEVEN

Westward by Train and Ship

It was 1966, the year of decimal currency. My annual leave came around and once again I had in my mind another visit to the Top End. This time I chose to go west to Perth. I got there on a variety of trains. The first was the Overland from Melbourne to Adelaide on the broad gauge route through Ballarat and Serviceton. From Adelaide the local train took me to Port Augusta passing through Port Pirie. At Port Augusta I boarded the Trans Continental train, the forerunner of the Indian Pacific. The Trans Continental travelled on standard gauge only as far as Kalgoorlie in those days. In the buffet car I discovered the difference in beers. Joining a small group of fellow travellers we sampled West End beer from Adelaide until it ran out, and then we were supplied with Hannans from Kalgoorlie. My observation was that it was a beer designed for thirsty, rugged and tough miners, not for genteel travellers from the east, but we survived.

At Kalgoorlie there was a three-hour wait until we could board the overnight Westland train which ran on the narrow gauge line to Perth. It left at nine o'clock that evening. During the day I had been extolling the pleasure of drinking rum and Coca-Cola, a habit I had picked up in Queensland. While waiting at Kalgoorlie I took several middle-aged ladies who had never tried the beverage to a nearby hotel. They appeared to enjoy the new tipple and we did make it back in time to board the Westland. It was a basic but comfortable train with well-made wooden carriages reflecting the skills of craftsmen decades before. The train had no heating so I felt the cold of inland Australia in July.

I had a week in Perth before heading north on the MV *Kabbarli,* one of the ships run by the Western Australian government to service coastal towns and settlements north from Perth to the Northern Territory with the voyage ending in Darwin. The *Kabbarli* and sister ships took everyday goods and passengers to these outposts before the days of road transport, providing a lifeline and public transport service. We left Perth with 38 passengers and holds full of goods needed to stock local stores. The journey took two weeks, with half-day stops at many of the Western Australian coastal towns.

We eventually arrived at Derby, north of Broome, just in time for the annual race meeting. The ship's purser said that we would be delayed a bit longer than usual because the watersiders would go on strike so that all could attend the race meeting. Sure enough, at mid-day, watched by the purser and me, the union representative came on deck, put his hand out and said it was far too wet to continue; work had to stop. There was not a cloud in the sky. No-one appeared concerned and a school bus was provided to take the passengers to the racecourse. The Derby racecourse in 1966 was a dirt course that had scrub growing in its centre. The horses, running anti-clockwise, ran along the straight from the start, disappeared behind the scrub in a cloud of dust and then emerged into the straight heading for the finish line. One of the passengers, a retired bookmaker, told me who was going to win by pointing out that there were four races with some of the horses ridden by four jockeys brought from Perth for the occasion. The most senior jockey would win the main race—and he did—and the other three would sort out the remaining results themselves. In the four races mentioned, the lead did not change once the horses emerged from behind the scrub and the ball of dust. The details had been worked out in the back straight out of sight. The other two races were for local amateur riders on stockhorses, one of which was a two-horse race. My bookmaker friend said it might be possible among the bookmakers to get odds of better than two to one on both horses. I didn't bother trying. There were five or six bookmakers operating and a totalisator. The tote appeared to be run by teenagers for the benefit of the local young people.

After the dust had settled and the races ended, the school bus picked up the passengers and we returned to the ship. Just before

Judge's box and bookmakers at Derby races, June 1966

the ship left, the police car pulled up and a youngish lady was escorted onto the ship by a policeman. After the ship sailed the journalist in me came out and I asked the lady in question why she had had a police escort. She was quite amiable about it and said she was a working girl who followed some of the race meetings around, providing solace for lonely stockmen who came in from stations for the races. In this case the policeman concerned was also looking for a bit of female company but was not prepared to pay for the pleasure. That led to the end of negotiations and the forced departure from Derby. I asked her how she would go in Darwin and she assured me she could look after herself. A few hours after arriving in Darwin I was walking along the main drag, Smith Street, and there was my lady sitting in a very expensive imported American sedan. As I walked past she smiled at me and gave me a thumbs up sign, a very professional woman.

After Derby our ship sailed through the waters of the Kimberley, passing the then newly developed mines on Cockatoo and Koolan Islands where large slabs of ores were being shipped overseas. The *Kabbarli* also brought supplies and people to these remote mining outposts. The last stop before Darwin was Wyndham, the most northerly Western Australian town. Another school bus took passengers to the new irrigation developments at Kununurra, centred around the Ord River inland from Wyndham. At that time there was a lot of optimism that the scheme would be a great success. That optimism was eventually tempered by the realities of local conditions and wildlife. The remainder of the voyage to Darwin was uneventful except that one night I joined in the bingo game and won about twenty games in succession. I placated the punters by shouting drinks all round, spending a good percentage of my winnings.

I had a week in Darwin and that introduced me to the old town before Cyclone Tracy destroyed a large part of it in 1974. I opted to stay at the Victoria Hotel in Smith Street in the heart of the town. It was one of the original hotels, built of stone, and has withstood cyclones and the Japanese bombing during the World War II. It cost $1.80 for a bed, there were two beds to each room and you took pot luck with your sleeping companion or paid double the price for privacy and the room to yourself. It was even cheaper if you chose a bed on the wide veranda. There were about ten beds lined up against the wall. When I first arrived those were the only beds available. About seven o'clock next morning one of the guests came onto the balcony in a pair of shorts with a truly well-filled gut hanging over them. He had a can of beer in his hand, which he drank, had a good burp and appeared ready for the day. Welcome to Darwin!

The saloon bar of the hotel, a rather makeshift affair with open sides and a tin roof, was on land next to the original building. The site is now occupied by shops and offices. I was sitting at a table when something swished past my head from behind. Natural preservation came into force and I dived under the table. From its safety I watched as an increasing space formed in the centre of the room as two ladies from the local indigenous population battled each other with handbags and fists. Judging by the colourful comments from the said ladies, the fight was over a young man who appeared not at all concerned over the fuss. The local constabulary arrived quickly (the station was just around the corner) but their enthusiasm to restore order quickly cooled as they saw who they had to deal with. Both gladiators soon ran out of puff and disappeared into the night, tables and chairs were set upright, glasses refilled and harmony returned. The male, the source of the fracas, stayed with his mates and had another drink.

Victoria Hotel, Smith Street, Darwin, August 1966

When I arrived in Darwin I vaguely knew one person, the head of the ABC newsroom. It's a friendly town and in the week I was there I went to two parties and one wedding reception. The perception that the Territory was a heterosexual male preserve was somewhat shattered at one party. There was a rather attractive man about my age who I started to earnestly chat up. The conversation didn't last too long as a giant of man, who looked as though he threw bullocks around for a living, uncurled himself from the floor and said 'Leave my boyfriend alone!' I am a pragmatist, and left his boyfriend alone. I happily survived that, the other party and the wedding reception which involved a member of the local ABC staff. I then had to head home as my leave was just about up. The return trip was, I am glad to say, uneventful. Two planes took me to Melbourne, via Alice Springs and Adelaide.

EIGHT

Around the World

Having seen a lot of Australia, at the age of 31, I thought it would be a good idea to see what other countries looked like. In March 1967 I booked a berth on the MV *Patris* leaving Australia a year later. The *Patris* was one of a number of the Greek Chandris line ships which brought migrants to Australia and offered cheap fares to Europe to attract passengers for the return journey. This meant no travel in 1967 as I saved up holiday pay, sold the car and offered to work any overtime available to stow away money to pay for the adventure. As I enjoyed my work and wanted to return to television news with the ABC on my return, I asked for extended leave without pay. Unfortunately for me this was turned down so on 13 April 1968 I resigned from the ABC.

Eight days later I boarded the *Patris* in Melbourne, and got my first shock. The ship was nearly at the end of its outward journey and had to continue to Sydney to deliver the last of the migrants. To take as many people as they could fit in, the ship's conditions were basic with no frills. In Sydney we were told to take the day off and the ship would look much better when we got back. They were much better; instead of 1500 migrants there were 900 paying passengers, curtains and carpets appeared over bare floors and individual tables replaced the long trestle tables in the dining room. From Sydney the *Patris* began its return voyage bypassing Melbourne, stopping at Adelaide and Fremantle to pick up more passengers.

As we sailed west in to the sunset (I think it was earlier in the day, but it sounds good), I watched the tall buildings of Perth and Fremantle disappear in the distance and wondered when or if I would see Australia again. Due to a stoush between France, England and Egypt the Suez Canal was filled with sunken ships so on this voyage we had to travel around the Cape of Good Hope, so the first stop was Cape Town in South Africa. Just out from Fremantle the first interesting time came with a lifeboat drill. The passenger list contained about 100 English-speaking travellers while the remainder were Greek Australians who had migrated many years before and were taking the opportunity to visit their old homeland. The first orders in the drill came in English and Greek directing my section to a certain lounge to await further instructions. These came through all right, but only in Greek. So we sat in this lounge listening to a whole lot of urgent calls in Greek. Eventually a flustered officer came to the lounge and wanted to know why we were still there, in Greek. He was told in robust Australian we couldn't understand a word of what was being said. It then dawned on him there were non-Greek speaking passengers aboard. We were ushered to our correct lifeboat and found it was the one the captain would also use. I wasn't sure about that – wasn't the captain supposed to be the last person to leave a sinking ship? From that point on all announcements came in English and Greek.

I also took the opportunity to attend daily classes in basic Greek which I found very useful later in my travels. Halfway across the Indian Ocean we ran in to my first storm at sea. Before leaving I had seen my doctor who not only organised the vaccinations I had to have, but also gave me some very good anti-seasickness pills which happily worked very well. That evening with the storm at its worst I was invited with another six people to dine at the captain's table. The seating arrangements were three guests on each side, the captain at one end and an officer at the other. There was a lot of movement as the ship battled the weather. Then there was a severe lurch, water glasses were spilled and with water on the floor the three of us, still sitting on our chairs, slid gracefully backwards into the next table, then the ship lurched the other way and we slid back to our table while the three guests on the other side of the table repeated the performance in reverse. It was a scene straight from an old silent movie. The reaction of the captain was immediate. He summoned a waiter to pass on some terse instructions, in Greek, to the officer on watch, and had a steward standing behind the chairs so that we could stay at the table to finish the meal. It also appeared that not all of the waiters had got their sea legs as dishes were served quickly by some who looked pale and grim-faced.

The ship safely arrived at Cape Town and I stepped on South African soil, my first time in a foreign country. I also saw the ugly reality of apartheid with signs in many places saying 'whites only', especially along the lovely beaches where the sandy parts were reserved for the whites and the black and coloured people had to make the best of rocky outcrops. However the only time I was approached for money was by a poor-looking white person. Apparently apartheid didn't work for everyone. Before leaving the ship to go ashore we were able to change some of our money into Rand but told not to bring it back because no one wanted the currency. I was with some of the non-Greek passengers having a look around the city. At the end of the day before boarding the ship to sail we decided the best way to get rid of our left over Rand was to try the local beer at a hotel near the wharf. We duly went in to the whites-only bar and had some fine samples of South African brewing. It was a very pleasant time and it passed quickly, just about too quickly, resulting in a very quick dash to the *Patris* to find the main gangplank had gone and the only one left was one at wharf level leading into the staff quarters. We made it with not much time to spare. I later wondered what I would have done next if I saw the ship sailing out of the harbour. I am not sure whether they were counting the passengers or not.

We then spent twelve days on board the ship as it sailed north to Gibraltar. During that time I continued my Greek language lessons and got to know some of the other passengers. These included a middle-aged woman who was wondering if I needed some personal comfort for a price. When I declined her teenage son came up with a similar offer. They had quickly worked out my preferences. I also declined his offer. It was also interesting to note that the Greek Australians returning to Greece were being more Greek than the Greeks. A lady attached to the Australian Immigration Department was travelling to Greece to accompany the next set of immigrants coming to Australia. She said these expatriates were going to be very disappointed when they return after a fifteen- or twenty-year absence as the country itself has changed so much after 1945.

The *Patris* had five engineers, or officers, but only needed four. I soon found out why the fifth engineer was on board. In 1967 a group of army colonels had overthrown the elected government and were running a dictatorship. The fifth engineer was there to keep eye on people coming into the country. I had 'journalist' as my occupation on official papers so I wasn't entirely surprised about being invited to parties in his cabin, along with other guests. Somehow or other, despite considerable amounts of Metaxa brandy, the local Greek spirit, at three o'clock in the morning (my guess) when I was asked very quietly by the engineer what I thought of the present political situations in Greece, I was able to say, more or less clearly, it was up to the Greeks to run their own country. The only event of note in the twelve days at sea was crossing the Equator when King Neptune 'came aboard' and I witnessed what I was told was a traditional ceremony that involved lewd jokes in English and Greek, an assortment of semi-naked young women and men, and carrots. The rest I leave to your imagination, not my description.

We eventually arrived in Gibraltar for a day. Later that year, Gibraltar was going to vote on whether to remain a British colony or become part of Spain. There was no doubt what the locals wanted judging by the Union Jacks flying everywhere. The Gibraltarians were even taking their enthusiasm to remain British to rather extreme measures. In good English fashion they were serving their beer at room temperature. In England, where beer comes from kegs in the cellar, it is not far off drinkable refrigerator level. Gibraltar is not far from the equator and with an outside temperature of 36°C the beer from the cellar kegs was lukewarm. Even one Englishman returning home couldn't drink it.

That same chap, after we sailed, showed us a watch he'd bought from a street vendor for £1.15. We started taking bets on when it would fall apart. Three months later I caught up with him at his home in England and the first thing he said to me on arrival was that 'It is still working', showing me the watch.

From Gibraltar we sailed to Naples in Italy where again we had a day free for sightseeing. From the moment we left the ship we were mobbed by earnest salesmen, even waiting at the end of the gangplank for our custom. I had dressed in a tailored shirt and coat and looked as if I had money. My companion, dressed in a very scruffy shirt and aged jeans, got quite different treatment. Within earshot, the same goodies I was being offered were presented to him at half the price, a special for the crew. I also found a use for my Greek. When replying in that language they lost interest as, I was told later, Italians believed that the Greeks weren't much use as customers since they had no money or wouldn't part with it. I remembered that when visiting Italy later on in this journey. Three of us, all reasonably young and fit males, visited some of the poorer suburbs on the steep slopes of Naples. It was a warm day and unlike Australia every little café sold cold beer. At one, this elderly lady became quite excited when she found out we were Australians. Her sons and daughters had migrated to Australia and she wanted to know more about the country. Her English was basic and our Italian was even worse but it was a very pleasant few minutes spent in her shop.

The final leg of the voyage was to Piraeus, the port for Athens. At Naples the Greek customs and immigration officials boarded the ship and went through the formalities and clearances so that there was no hold-up on arrival. The fifth engineer then presented himself in his proper role standing behind the officials assisting them with any extra information they needed. When it came to my turn, they quickly turned to him as they found I was a journalist. After a short time and some explanation in Greek I was given the thumbs-up metaphorically, and had my passport stamped. The hangovers from the brandy had been worthwhile. As part of our ticket we could stay two nights on board the *Patris* which gave me free accommodation while sightseeing.

From Athens my plans were to travel through Europe by train and then sail back to Australia by way of the Americas taking another seven months. By that time the money would have run out. I had budgeted on how much I was prepared to spend a day, for instance a maximum of $4 a night for accommodation, $3 for travel and about $2 on food. Remember, these were 1968 prices. When I arrived at a railway station I went to the tourist information desk, if there was one, and got free details on public transport and hotels. If the necessary information was not available, I would then walk from the station to the nearest hotel which didn't have a uniformed porter in front (guess who pays for the uniforms) and ask how much a room was. If the quote was too high, I politely said it was beyond my budget. If they asked what was my budget, I would tell them in local currency and many times the hotel did have available a little room which would suit me. Tourists were in short supply in many areas in those days and no one knocked back bums in beds. The hotels that included a breakfast were a bonus. When eating I avoided cafes in tourist areas and those which did not have their menus displayed. This often took me to places off the beaten track and when you are hungry and no one speaks English, you learn the local language very quickly.

With my two days in Athens I took in ancient Greece, or what was left of it, and felt confident the Greek colonels weren't interested in this particular journalist. Using my new-found skills in Greek I also managed to buy a rail ticket to Salonika in the north of the country. The main town in between is Larissa where I stayed overnight. Halfway between Athens and Larissa is Lamia. The train arrived about five minutes late and I watched the guard being escorted by two uniformed officers to the locomotive presumably to find an explanation for the tardiness of the train. Were the colonels trying to emulate Mussolini and get Greek trains running on time? The train eventually arrived safely in Larissa with no dead bodies in sight. From Salonika my next part of the journey took me through what was then Yugoslavia, the communist state under the control of the dictator Tito.

The first night in Yugoslavia was in Skopje, now the capital of Macedonia. Here I experienced the stifling effect of a socialist bureaucracy. First I had to book in at the tourist hotel, no options but within the budget. I was fed there, within the budget, then early in the evening I walked to the central square where hundreds of people appeared to be wandering around with nothing to do, no advertising signs and it appeared no shops open, all very gloomy and dismal. Next day I travelled on to the capital Belgrade, now the Serbian capital. At the station I tried to get a bed at a hotel nearby but was told foreigners had to go to the tourist hotel some blocks away. When I got there I was told by the clerk, who could speak English quite well, that there was nothing available. He appeared to be a well-educated person and I'm guessing he had a fairly important job before the communists took over, and now survived because he could speak English and possibly other languages. I managed to find a place to eat and, with no other option, headed for the railway station looking for the next train to Austria. I gave up all hope of seeing more of Yugoslavia. I had failed to plan in advance and no socialist dictatorship was going to have tourists wandering around unsupervised.

The next train to Graz in southern Austria left at about four o'clock the next morning, so the night was spent on a less than comfortable railway seat. The armed guard patrolling the empty station made me change seats a couple of times. I am not sure why. I couldn't understand Serbo-Croat and I am pretty sure he couldn't understand English. I felt he wasn't aggressive but wasn't sure what to do with this foreigner who had a British passport marked 'Australia'. (These documents preceded today's Australian passport with our coat of arms. My first one had the British coat of arms.) The train duly arrived more or less on time, hauled by a shiny black steam locomotive with a big red star on the front.

At the Austrian border, customs officials entered our carriage where one of the passengers had a bottle of what appeared to be wine. She was told she could not bring it into Austria but she could drink it on the spot. So she opened the bottle and passed it around the compartment. I thought it was home-made wine and, not having had a drink for a while, took a good mouthful. It was a home-made brandy-type spirit. I resumed breathing shortly afterwards and thank goodness there were no further ill effects. On crossing the Austrian border the bright colours of a Shell service station were in direct contrast to the greys and blacks of a 'workers' paradise'.

Further pleasure awaited me when I arrived in Vienna. After a day of sightseeing I went for a stroll on a warm spring night to a nearby park to be greeted by an orchestra playing Strauss waltzes on an open-air stage. It was a great welcome to Austria where I had a chance to brush up on my German. In the previous year I decided it would be a good idea to have some knowledge of a language other than English. I chose German, working on the theory that a good part of central Europe spoke some form of it and it was related to English. This learning opportunity came when I had a series of long shifts on Sundays when someone was needed on duty in case something newsworthy happened. I took the time to teach myself basic German from a teach yourself book. Being in Austria I took the opportunity to try my linguistic skills on unsuspecting locals. With practice I was able to converse in a limited way. Later in Germany I was told I spoke with an Austrian accent.

Omnibus train, Schwarzach, Austria, June 1968

After several days visiting some of the beautiful cities in eastern Austria I took the train from Salzburg to Innsbruck. I purposely took the omnibus, the slow train that stops at every station mainly for the benefit of local people going from one village to the next. When we pulled up at one large station the conductor suggested I get off and get the next train, an express that would get me to Innsbruck faster. I told him I was happy to look at the countryside and I wasn't in a hurry. He got the message and at several stops he told me the train was there for fifteen minutes and to get out and see the village. He said he would make sure the train would wait until I got back. I never did try it, but I have a feeling the train, of only two carriages, would have waited. After admiring the lofty peaks surrounding Innsbruck I continued my journey west on the train to Zurich which travels through the Tyrol valley. I got off at a small village called Schaan, the only railway station in the Principality of Liechtenstein.

I planned to stay a few days in this small remnant of the Holy Roman Empire. The proprietor of the hotel near the station warmly greeted this Australian journalist and proudly showed me the four newspapers printed in his country which, considering the small population, was quite an achievement. I was also told about the big fund-raising beer festival next day at Balzers, the most southern village in the country just 16 kilometres south of Schaan. Liechtenstein is on the east side of the Danube River which forms the border with Switzerland. The easiest way to get there was to walk. This took me through the capital Vaduz, only four kilometres from Schaan, and then onto Balzers. The beer fest was to raise funds for the fire brigade, a mainly volunteer organisation taking care of all emergency situations. There was a very large tent with tables and chairs, and two bands, one playing traditional music and the other the latest rock. There were stalls selling foods, and women dressed in traditional tavern costumes selling and serving large steins of beer. The guest of honour was the wife of the Crown Prince, Princess Georgina, who arrived by car in the front passenger seat and was greeted by the local policeman who opened the car door and saluted. As she walked into the tent everyone stood and a band played the Liechtenstein national anthem, the same tune as 'God save the Queen' that is an old Germanic tune from the time of the Hanoverians. A good time was had by all including yours truly. On the departure of

Beerfest tent, Balzers, Liechtenstein, June 1968

HRH Princes Georgina arriving, Balzers, Liechtenstein, June 1968

the Crown Princess balloons were released in celebration of the birth of a grandson who was then second in line to the throne. As they drifted high in the air south towards communist Yugoslavia with this celebration of monarchy printed on the balloons, I contemplated the reaction of the fervid socialists.

The next day after recovering from the excesses (limited, probably just as well, by budget) of the fest, I walked to Vaduz and took the Royal Liechtenstein Mail coach to Malbun, the most eastern village, or commune, in the Principality some ten kilometres from the capital. To get there the bus winds up a narrow one-lane road over a mountain range before reaching Malbun in a small valley. In the Principality, the Royal Liechtenstein Mail has precedence. On one bend, the Royal Mail met an Italian tourist bus which had to reverse to the nearest passing point. It did, straight into a car driven by a German tourist. Both drivers got out to sort the problem in a mixture of Italian and German while our driver turned off the Royal Mail coach's engine, got out his newspaper and waited for the other vehicles to make way for the Mail. Apparently this was a not uncommon occurrence. Not much damage was done to the two vehicles and both backed back to a passing point allowing the Royal Liechtenstein Mail to proceed in its customary manner. At Malbun, I took a ski lift to the top of a nearby mountain giving me a view of four countries, Austria to the east, Yugoslavia to the south, Switzerland to the west and Germany to the north. No traffic to worry about on the return trip.

The next day I farewelled my host at my little hotel in Schaan and boarded the train to Zurich. On boarding European trains, it is necessary to look at the destination sign on the side of the carriage door as quite often trains divide at some junction stations with a section of the train going in one direction while the other carriages went to another city. I arrived in Zurich as planned. Switzerland is a quiet country with some lovely tourist attractions and my visit was again interesting and quiet; everything went as it should, like a Swiss clock. On the way south to Milan in Italy the train went through the Simplon tunnel. There was a very steep descent at the mouth of the tunnel down into the valley where we stopped at Kanderstag to allow the brakes on the train to cool down. From the carriage window I could see the steam coming from each wheel.

From Milan I was the perfect tourist, travelling east to eventually arrive in Rimini on the east coast. Being intrigued by small countries I took the bus from Rimini to the Republic of San Marino, another leftover from the city republics of past centuries. It was easy to see why the country had remained independent. On its northern border a sheer cliff face rises from the plain while a river and steep terrain made it easy to defend from the other approaches. On a rare occasion while travelling, out of the blue comes a brief love affair. As I was doing my tourist bit I started talking to a very attractive young man who suggested we go to one of the taverns on the top of the cliff face, with a magnificent view, and try the local brandy. Who could refuse such an offer? He was a tourist bus driver from Finland who had sent his passengers off for a couple of hours to enjoy the sights and sounds of San Marino and boost the local economy. After enjoying several glasses of the local spirits he had to collect his passengers but we agreed to meet that night in the hotel he was staying at Riggionni, some 20 kilometres south of Rimini and connected by a trolley bus service. I dutifully left my boarding house and took the bus to Riggionni and met up with my friend. After a mutually pleasant night I got the bus back to Rimini arriving at the boarding house at about six o'clock in the morning to be met by a very irate night porter who had waited up all night for me to return. I apologised as best I could in rather shattered Italian and pointed out that no one told me there would be anyone waiting for me to return.

City towers, San Marino, June 1968

I quietly fled Rimini the next day, taking the train to Foggia and then west on to Naples. In Switzerland I had purchased a special tourist ticket for Italy which allowed me to use Italian trains at any time. It was supposed to be for second-class travel but it appears no one had told the train conductors about that and when I used it inadvertently in a first-class carriage it passed inspection. From then on I used the less crowded first-class carriages. On the train to Foggia I took the remaining seat in a compartment. The other seven seats were filled by middle-aged Italians with the traditional day's growth on their faces, reminding me of films about Italian criminals. Unafraid and undaunted I put my case on the rack and sat down. One of the men in very basic English asked if I was Australian (he had seen an Australian label on the case). I said, 'Si', and he said, 'You know Sydney?' I replied that I did. He then said, 'I have a cousin in Sydney, you know my cousin?' I explained as best I could that Sydney was a big city and it would be unusual for me to know his cousin. He then spoke to his companions in Italian, smiled, added a few more words, and then produced, in quick succession, a rather large knife and some bread rolls. Out from a bag came some pre-cooked meats of unknown origin which were sliced and placed in the rolls, and one was handed to me. I smiled, accepted the roll, thanked them and bit into it. I thought to myself I haven't the faintest idea what I'm eating but here goes. When in Italy do as the Italians do. It was OK.

In Naples the usual band of street vendors and peddlers of the usual exotic range of services appeared at the railway station and once again my Greek came to my assistance as they looked around for more compliant prey. When I arrived in Rome the thought struck me as I wandered through the remains of the old Roman state: what would our modern cities look like in four thousand years' time? Will our modern towers of steel and glass be still there, or just some rusting steel skeletons, reminders of some past civilisation?

In Pisa I climbed the leaning tower and walked around the top balcony which does lean. It gives you a good view of the city but on the down side it was a bit scary as there were no hand rails. By now I had settled in to a routine tourist schedule, visiting the right spots at the right time. In the French Riviera I stopped briefly in the Principality of Monaco. Admiring the yachts at the quay in Monte Carlo I pondered the thought of becoming a gigolo to make use of some of the excess wealth that was evident, reflected by the magnificent yachts moored in the harbour. I decided I would have a longer working life as a journalist.

In Nice I briefly held up the rush of commuters as I passed through the station ticket barrier. The handle on my suitcase broke and I had to lever the thing through the barrier and half carried it or pulled it to the nearest hotel (within budget). I replaced it with two cases half the size and much easier to handle as I could walk reasonably balanced instead of being lopsided with one heavy suitcase. In 1968 there were no suitcases on wheels, an invention I now approve. I was ready to admire the famous Nice foreshore so well publicised. To my surprise not a speck of sand in sight, only grey pebbles stretching into the water. My romantic visions of the French Riviera came crashing down.

Remaining in the south of France, I spent Bastille Day at Montpellier. I joined in the celebrations early in the evening in the main city square then retired to my hotel near the station. Barriers had been put across some of the streets to keep cars away from revellers in the square including one barrier outside my hotel. At four in the morning someone, who might have been partying, drove through it and then continued on his/her merry way.

Fleeing the festivities of the French I travelled south the next day into Spain and after changing trains at Barcelona headed to Zaragoza. The day was hot and the second-class carriage was filled to capacity, including a woman with three children. For some reason the train stopped in the countryside for an hour or more and the children were getting hungry and thirsty. Mum brought out some hard-boiled eggs, shelled them (shells on the floor) and gave them to the children. A combination of the smell of hard-boiled eggs, a hot day, and a very crowded carriage with no air-conditioning was certainly a tough test for the hardy and not so hardy traveller. I, along with some of the other travellers, made for the open windows in the corridor.

Eventually the train arrived in the evening at Zaragoza. At the station I was approached by a man who wanted to know if I wanted a bed for the night. I was a bit doubtful but it was dark and I didn't know where the nearest hotel was. I accepted the offer. He led me through several small back streets to his building and flat on the third floor. His wife took my details and asked for my passport. She looked at it and disappeared into the next room, calling out 'Australian'. Out came a young, very pregnant lady, and I thought, 'What on earth did the last Australian do here?' She smiled and in good Australian said 'G'day mate'. After regaining my equilibrium and being shown my room, she told me she came from Sydney. She had met her husband, the son of the landlord there, had married and decided to have the baby in Zaragoza. Apparently the facilities were good and cheap and the baby would have dual citizenship. The husband's family made extra money by taking in paying guests. I had a wonderful night with her catching up on events in Australia. In the morning I enjoyed a traditional breakfast of goats' milk and home-made bread plus some fruit. All within budget. The next morning the landlord showed me the way back to the station through the maze of little streets so I could get the train to Madrid.

My preferred train to the Spanish capital was again the one that stopped all stations. It took all day travelling at a gentle pace. It also meant there was plenty of room. At about midday the train arrived at Arcos de Jalon, about halfway to the destination. The conductor said the train would be there for nearly two hours but I could stay on board. As it was quite hot I decided I would do what the locals did in the heat of the noonday sun and have a siesta. I stretched out across the bench seats and relaxed. At the time Spain was still under the rule of the dictator, General Franco. Shortly after I settled in for a snooze, I could hear the tread of military boots and saw a soldier carrying a rifle passing the compartment. I wondered what was going to happen next. He looked in, saw I was half asleep and, respecting the Spanish tradition of the siesta, tip-toed quietly away. I had a good sleep under the care of the army.

Zaragoza–Madrid mail train, Arcos de Jolon, Spain November 1968

In Madrid there was little sign of a heavy police or military presence, but I did go to an area where I had learnt that during the civil war in the late 1930s people had been executed. Sure enough, thirty years later, there was still a line of bullet holes in a wall at about chest height where the people had been shot. Moving onto Lisbon, in Portugal, there were more signs of the tyrannical reign of its dictator, President Salazar. The first day I was there I saw a large group of police put a road block across one of the main streets and check every drivers' papers. A similar experience happened to me the following night. At about one o'clock in the morning I was in bed on the third floor of my cheap boarding house. There was loud banging on the front door, a lot of talk in Portuguese and then the clump of military boots going from room to room waking the inhabitants. As the entourage approached my room I grabbed my passport and put it under the pillow, tried to remember the address of the Australian consulate, and waited. Outside my room I heard the landlady speaking in Portuguese to the group and the only words I could make out was 'tourist' and 'Australian'. That satisfied them and they moved on. I did the right thing and went back to sleep.

Lisbon had a tram system, and I was intrigued by the way the trams wound their way through some of the narrow streets in the city centre. On the broader streets there were two tram lines. When the tram came to the narrow streets the lines became one. Halfway along, the one line turned into another narrow street before turning again to the larger street where the lines returned as each-way tracks. At each corner there was a man with a red or green flag who would signal to the man on the next corner if a tram was on the single line. No automated signals but certainly a way of providing jobs.

On the outskirts of Lisbon there were forests of Australian eucalypts planted for the hardwood. The locals called them the Australian weed, so I was told. Seeing the gum trees made me a little homesick. It was hot and I was more than a little thirsty. Near the forest was a little group of shops and a young man beckoned me and using sign language wondered if I needed a drink. I nodded and was led down to an underground tavern with large casks of wine sticking out from the wall. For the equivalent of five cents Australian I was given a large glass of cold white wine, very enjoyable and a nice surprise. The young man was the proprietor's son whose job appeared to be to lure tourists to the tavern.

I survived the dictatorship of Portugal and travelling north arriving in the French city of Bordeaux. To get to Paris I took the Express, which in those days did the 600-kilometre journey in six hours with several stops thrown in. Fifty years later in Australia there is still no train that goes that fast. I shared the compartment with a young lady who spoke far better English than my schoolboy French. She had been visiting her aunt who lived in a small village in the Pyrenees. Fearful of the perils of starvation for her niece on the long journey to Paris, the good lady had provided a hamper of food that would have done justice to an Australian Rules football team. She was happy to share the hamper with me and to reciprocate I bought a bottle of wine at the next station. As the train arrived at each station a swarm of sellers with handcarts would go beside the carriages offering food and local wines for sale which I thought was very civilised. Needless to say it was a very pleasant trip to Paris and I certainly did not have to buy a meal that night. I spent several days in Paris and had another love affair, this time with the city itself. Its charm, its vitality and the people – once they found out you were not British or American. A kangaroo badge helped, but I avoided the Australian flag badge. The Union Jack on the corner was not helpful.

The next stage of the odyssey was the ferry from Calais in France to Dover in England. At the bar on the ferry I got talking to a Canadian soldier on leave from his base in Germany. He was making up for the lack of good strong drink not available while on duty. As the beverages were duty free, I was happy to join him. By the time we arrived at Dover I was even happier. At the border check my new companion declared that I was too drunk to be admitted, proving also that his condition wasn't much better. The official quickly checked our passports and appeared to be very happy to get rid of these two drunks from the colonies.

Of the five days that I stayed in London in early August, it rained for four of them, then came along the one day of summer when the clouds parted and the sun shone. This was the day the English got their tan. Never have I seen a sight like it, hundreds of lily-white bodies of all shapes and sizes and with the minimum of clothing, sunbaking in the parks. It was quite a fascinating sight.

On my way north through England I arrived in Grantham where I was met by a friend of my mother who lived nearby at a village called Foston. She had invited me to stay for a couple of days which included some sightseeing trips around the county. She was a delightful lady in her sixties who lived in a stone house built in the sixteenth century. In those days people must have been shorter because I had to duck my head to go through every doorway. She also made her own wine from various locally grown fruit and vegetables, and invited me to taste some of her products. There was parsnip wine, strawberry wine, and so on. They all had some strength in them because towards the end of the tastings I found it necessary to hold up a wall or two as I staggered around the house. There appeared to be no effect on the maker. I slept well that night and there were no after-effects the following morning.

After that enjoyable break I made my way eventually to Edinburgh in Scotland just in time for the famous military tattoo. My first introduction was standing on the ramparts of Edinburgh Castle watching and listening to massed pipe bands marching in the valley below along High Street. The spectacle was magnificent, and I was able to get a ticket for the Tattoo the following night. Two scenes remain in my mind: the pipe bands in kilts marching from the Castle onto the forecourt, and at the end the lone piper playing the lament on the Castle wall. Visions like that remain forever in your mind.

Venturing further into Scotland I arrived at Aberdeen on the North Sea on the day the Soviet army invaded Czechoslovakia, 20 August 1968. There was quite a lot of tension in the air as people wondered what was going to happen next. This was increased as RAF fighter jets screamed overhead up and down the coastline for two days.

The third World War was averted and so I continued my meanderings around Scotland, ending up in Glasgow just in time to watch from a distance a scaled-down version of a good barney (Australian for fight). I was admiring the historic Glasgow University when two gangs of youth approached each other on the lawns between the University and the river. An all-in melee broke out and lasted for quite a few minutes. It hadn't gone unnoticed as the sounds of police sirens in the distance could be heard. As the first police cars approached, the combatants melted into nearby streets. Four police cars came in from all sides, going around in circles on the now empty lawns.

Leaving feuding Scots to themselves I came south to Liverpool to board the ferry to Ireland. Most of the cheap accommodation I had stayed in throughout Europe had been well presented and clean. I can't say that about the dump I ended up in in Liverpool. In the bed and breakfast place I pulled back the blankets preparing for sleep. I wasn't the first one to sleep between those same sheets, nor possibly the second or third. I pulled the blankets back again and spent the night fully clothed on the top blanket, having covered the pillow with what looked like a clean towel. No use complaining.

A ferry took me across the Irish Sea from Liverpool to Dublin and once again the duty-free bar attracted my attention so I was in a fairly jovial frame of mind as I stepped ashore. A colleague of mine at work had written to his parents in Dublin telling of my coming and as a result I was invited to meet his family. I then had my first introduction to Irish hospitality. After a very pleasant and filling meal at their place my colleague's sister and her boyfriend suggested we visit a pub which had a good Irish band. We had a good time but closing time was ten o'clock and this pub closed at the legal hour. I was told not to worry, there was a pub that was run by the sister of the Minister of Justice and that would be open, and it was until the wee hours.

Much later that day I was in O'Connell Street at a major intersection where a policeman was directing traffic. Two very attractive young ladies wearing brief miniskirts, a new fashion in those days, walked to the policeman in the centre of the intersection to ask directions. He smiled, stopped the traffic in all directions, and in an easygoing manner eventually pointed them in the right direction. He then signalled traffic to resume as usual. Not one car horn sounded and no drivers showed any sign of impatience. Miniskirted maidens must have been an unusual sight. As I enjoy a glass or three of stout, a visit to the Guinness Brewery was a must and the enjoyment began about a block away as the aroma of freshly brewed stout pervaded the atmosphere, and despite the previous evening of Irish hospitality I felt no pain from the experience.

Using a variety of trains, some modern and some well and truly from the 1930s, I criss-crossed the south of the Republic and arrived in Tralee unintentionally in time for the Rose of Tralee festival. That evening I joined in the festivities, met a chap (which developed into a longstanding friendship over many years), and left the pub at two o'clock in the morning, well past the legal closing time. A couple of days later I read with interest the way the government dealt with this breach of the law and I quote from memory, not verbatim, what appeared in the local press. 'Due to the fact that the extended closing time of one o'clock for pubs for the Rose of Tralee festival was ignored, next year the pubs will be allowed to stay open until two o'clock in the morning.' Good grief, a government actually doing what the people wanted.

On the west coast of Ireland Gaelic is a familiar language and in Limerick I got a street map of the town with the street names all in English. When I began my walking tour of the town I found that all the street signs were in Gaelic and there was no connection between the two languages. Luckily such landmarks as the cathedral, post office and railway station were marked so I used them as guides. I also found that it was very easy to understand the locals who spoke English with a broad Irish accent. I suspect that the Australian accent was developed from both an Irish and Cockney source, probably due to the fact our predecessors in the prison ships came from these two areas. When I reached Galway on my way to Sligo I had to change from train to bus and once again I ran into the language problem. At the bus terminal all the destination signs on the buses were in Gaelic so with the help of a guide book I found the right bus by comparing the name in Gaelic and English in the guide book to the Gaelic sign on the bus, and yes, I did arrive as planned in Sligo.

I found a bed and breakfast for the night. On my travels there were few places that had showers in the bathroom and if you wanted a bath you had to pay for it. That was the case here and as the cost for the night was below budget I paid the landlady five shillings for the privilege of a luxurious bath. It looked the size of small swimming pool. I really enjoyed it and wallowed for some time. After a huge breakfast the next day – nothing like Irish hospitality – I took the bus, with the sign in English, to Enniskillen in Northern Ireland.

1968 was the year before the Troubles broke out between Catholics and Protestants. Apart from the religious bitterness I believe there was also an economic conflict between the 'haves' and the 'have nots. As I crossed the border there was no sign of problems when two British customs officials boarded the bus, chatted to the driver, ignored the passengers, looked under the back seat of the bus and left. In Londonderry the tension was evident when I walked into a pub close to my bed and breakfast. I was a stranger, so the place fell silent and one of the customers asked, 'Are you a "proddy" or one of us?' In other pubs during my stay in Ulster, the provincial name for Northern Ireland, the query could also be 'Are you a "Mick" or one of us?' In all cases my reply was, with a broad Australian accent, 'I don't know what you're talking about, mate, I'm Australian.' From then on there was no problem; they didn't care whether I was Catholic, Jew, Protestant or Muslim. It also appeared that every Irishman north or south had a relative in Australia.

In Belfast I saw another sign of the coming problems. There was a park which had a tor or rugged hill and I thought that from the top I could get some good photos of the city. I took a track that wound through scrub and, near the top, came out into a little clearing where a group of men armed with pistols were having target practice. I was pretty sure this was not a social pistol club and having in mind what I had already noticed, I did an about-turn very discreetly and retreated into the scrub and down the hill. After the tensions of Ulster I was happy to return to the Republic.

Crossing the border at Drogheda the passengers on the train, if not British or Irish, had to pass through customs. There were few on the train that came into that category and there was only one customs man on duty. I was next behind an American woman who was bitterly complaining about having her case opened. The more she complained the more the customs officer searched her luggage, took the contents out then eventually he stuffed them all back in the bag and let her go. I was next and he said to me, 'I don't know what all the fuss was about, my job is to open the case.' With that he unzipped my case and then zipped it up again and I was free to enter Ireland. I said goodbye to the Republic with a ferry from Dublin to Holyhead in Wales. This time my companion in the duty-free bar was another Commonwealth citizen, this time from Singapore. We arrived in a rather jolly condition, as the English would say.

Having a look at the west of England I took a train that ran through the Welsh hills from Shrewsbury to Cardiff passing through villages with those long Welsh names including the longest one in Britain which I did not note, but I have one recorded, Llangammarch, which was nestled in a picturesque valley.

On my return to Britain my thoughts were about getting back to Australia. I had an open ticket to return on a Chandris line ship from Greece which would go back the same way as I came. The thought of returning on the more spartan migrant ship also did not appeal. I also wanted to return via the Americas so I found I could get a berth on the P. & O. liner, the *Orsova*. This would cost more money, more than I had, so, like all good sons, I asked Mum for money which she provided at five per cent interest. From the beginning she had taught me about the value of money, a lesson that has been very valuable all my life.

However I had a bit more touring to do before setting sail for home. This took me through southern England including the port city of Southampton where I saw a fleet of ocean liners berthed waiting to sail, before I reached Dover to get the ferry to Oostende in Belgium. Yes, there was a duty-free bar on the ferry; no more needs to be said.

In Brussels I got my room through the tourist desk at the railway station. The system was that they booked you in by phone then gave you directions to get to the accommodation. I was given an address and a tram and stop number, and had to be there within the hour or the booking was cancelled. I got there fairly promptly and was met by the landlady who told me the room was not ready yet as two young chaps who had booked it the night before had just left but I could leave my cases in it. She opened the room and saw that a wardrobe had been moved to allow two single beds to be put together. She looked at the scene and then, quite amused, said, 'All that trouble for just one night.' I compared that to the reaction of purse-lipped landladies at home in the 1960s.

In the Netherlands I admired the way the centre of Rotterdam had been rebuilt after being bombed heavily by both the British and the Germans, depending on who occupied the city at the time, during World War II. I was also lucky to run into a young man who took pride in his city and spent a couple of hours driving me around showing how the city had recovered. For those who are wondering if he was a nice young man, I will leave it at that.

In Amsterdam I had my first glimpse of the liberal Dutch attitude to censorship. I had left an Australia where politicians were frothing at the mouth over any form of nudity and immoral writing. In one of the main streets I saw my first bookshop where all these forbidden sights were on full display. I felt a bit guilty looking at them in case one of my relatives saw me perving and would tell Mum. So much for a politically and religiously inspired guilt upbringing. After leaving Amsterdam I visited the Netherlands Radio and Television Network at Hilversum, equivalent to the ABC in Australia, and was shown over the studios. Before leaving Australia I had asked if I could visit the complex and was invited. After the tour I was taken to lunch and enjoyed what I was told was a traditional vegetarian meal.

I ended my visit to the Netherlands at Eindhoven from where took a train through a slice of France to the Grand Duchy of Luxembourg. At the border the green French locomotive was replaced by a brilliant orange one of the Luxembourg national railways. I saw the ramparts on the Alzette River in the capital, Luxembourg de Ville, where a brave but hopelessly outnumbered Luxembourg army held up the German panzer advance on Belgium and France for one day in 1940 until Hitler threatened to blast the city out of existence if the country didn't surrender.

At Koblenz in what was then West Germany I took a train south along the Rhine to Mainz. I shared the compartment with a German army soldier and his guard dog. He tried out his English on me and I practiced my German. The dog's job was to stand at the door of the compartment at each stop and look ferocious. It was one way of having the apartment to ourselves. I learnt more about post-war Germany. In Mainz it turned out that there was a lack of public toilets; at least it felt like that as I was looking for a place for relief. To make matters worse, the city seemed to have fountains on every corner. Not really what one was looking for at that moment.

In Heidelberg my accommodation was away from the tourist area and near a student beer cellar straight from *The Student Prince*. The young people were from the nearby university, were very friendly and certainly enjoyed their beer. Munich was preparing for the 1972 Olympic Games and that made touring a bit difficult as an underground railway system was being built, which meant tearing up and closing some streets and parks. Travelling north from Munich a week later I was in Hamburg where I saw the German side of destruction of World War II where, like Coventry in England, the bombed-out cathedral ruins remain as a memorial of the stupidity and brutality of conflict.

The train north to Denmark terminated at Flensburg where I had to get a bus to Esbjerg. Originally the line continued through to Esbjerg and Hitler used it to bring his army in to conquer Denmark but at the end of the war the Danish tore it up so it could not be used that way again. I believe it has now been restored. The bus that usually carries local people from one town to another was delayed while the customs officer worked out what to do about a passenger with an Australian passport. All the other passengers, most of them known to the officials, were quickly checked, so I was the centre of curiosity as my passport disappeared into the office while I presume a phone call was made to headquarters. Soon the officer returned handed me my passport and with a smile said in good English, 'Welcome to Denmark.'

The afternoon train from Esbjerg to Odense was filled with school children who by then had English as a compulsory subject. Apparently not many English-speaking visitors used the train so as soon as they knew I could speak English they were not shy in putting their English to the test and I enjoyed being able to help. It was a very quick and fun journey. By the time I arrived in Copenhagen it was the beginning of November and I was feeling the cold. One day the top temperature was 4°C, and my wardrobe was designed for Australian not European winters. Continued travelling became mentally as well as physically tiring. I was finding I was not appreciating the sights I was seeing because my mind was finding it difficult to comprehend the uniqueness. I was glad to head south and took the train from Copenhagen to Lübeck in Germany. At Kykobing the train, filled with passengers, boarded the ferry to Lübeck. While the train was shunted onto the ferry the carriage doors were locked but once on board the carriage doors were unlocked and people could make their way to the duty-free bar. The four young people in my compartment did just that and we had a good time. Then we had to return to the carriage before disembarking but we left it too late; the carriage doors were locked.

We had to find our carriage as the train was going to be split at Lübeck with carriages going in different directions. One carriage looked just like the other, so a bit of panic. Then someone opened a window for us and with a bit of help from all around we all boarded through the window. Nothing like being young and fit. Luckily I found my compartment and bags, so they stayed with me instead of ending up goodness only knows where.

Within a week after travelling through Germany, Belgium and France I was at the port of Le Havre to board the liner *Orsova*. Not before time, I thought, since the first snows of winter were falling in Germany as I travelled between Cologne and Brussels. On schedule the *Orsova* arrived and on 14 November I was on my way home. I shared the cheapest cabin on the ship with three other young Australian males all returning from various trips around Europe. Today they would be termed 'backpackers', an unfamiliar term in 1968. They were a good mob and several times we shared on-shore excursions at various ports. I also enjoyed the luxury of not having to find a room for the night or something to eat during the day. This helped me recover from the stress of continued travelling over the last seven months.

Orsova *at Port Everglades, Florida, November 1968*

Our first port of call was Bermuda in the West Indies. Halfway across the Atlantic we ran into, to me, a fearsome North Atlantic storm. I was first aware of this when I woke up in the morning feeling quite bit of movement by the ship. On the advice of my local doctor I took the anti-seasickness pills I had been given before I left Australia, waited half an hour and then went for breakfast in the fairly empty dining room. I then ventured on deck to sample the full fury of the storm. As I watched a huge wave crash across and bury the bow of the liner, I decided this was not what I really wanted to see and hastened back inside to the comfort of one of the lounges.

After visiting West Indian ports the ship berthed at Fort Lauderdale near Miami in Florida. I had met up with several American tourists on board, one of whom was disembarking. He decided to show some of the people he had met on the voyage around Miami and the Everglades, a huge wetland near Miami. He did it in style by hiring a brilliant huge, white Lincoln convertible. Not only did we see the Everglades but also ended up drinking cocktails on the top floor of a Miami hotel. After travelling through Europe I had not been impressed with the behaviour and even arrogance of American tourists, but on their home soil they were completely different, friendly and courteous. Maybe I had run into the wrong ones in Europe.

Hire car and party, Everglades, Florida, November 1968

Going through that engineering marvel the Panama Canal I witnessed true British tradition at its best. In one of the locks we waited beside a Royal Navy submarine going the other way. The *Orsova* sounded its siren and raised the naval ensign and I watched as a sailor came out of the conning tower with a flag under his arm, ran to the flagpole at the end of the submarine, unfurled the ensign and saluted, to be greeted by another blast from the ship's siren. All very British. The empire lives on.

In Panama City I joined forces with my cabin companions and visited the city. Our taxi driver had a rather battered 'Yank tank' as we called them then, and drove from the port at breakneck speed on an eight-lane highway. I don't think he ever once looked at the road; he was more interested in trying to sell us a range of exotic pleasure he had available. Girls were the first on his list and as we showed little interest the offers became even more varied and exotic. My companions, like myself, had little spare cash for such purchases after our travels. We arrived safely in the town centre more by good luck than anything else judging by the state of the taxi. We wandered around the streets including the real slum areas, intrigued by the crowded three- or four-storey tenement houses and their dilapidated appearance. We had changed some money for Panamanian dollars which no locals wanted to accept from foreigners. Before boarding the ship we decided to use up the local currency at a tavern. We started a conversation with a local businessman later and told him where we had gone. He looked horrified and said we could have got ourselves killed as the area concerned was notorious for murder and crime. I suspect that the sight of four solidly built and fit young men was enough to deter any random attack. The ship's management had told us where we could get a bus at a certain time to take us back to the

Orsova. The bus, with no glass in its windows and a line of bullet holes along the side, did turn up as promised. There had been a coup a few months before.

We had teamed up with two chaps from San Francisco who had joined the ship in the Bahamas for a short cruise before returning home. At Acapulco in Mexico they wanted to get one dozen bottles of tequila to bring back. Our cabin steward from Goa, then the Portuguese settlement in India, told us where to buy tequila at half the price of the cost at the tourist spots. He would like a bottle for himself for the information. We duly did as he suggested. It was half the price and our steward got his bottle. He must have enjoyed it as we had to make our own beds and tidy the cabin for the next two days. At San Francisco our two American friends disembarked but they had a problem. They could only bring in one bottle of tequila each, duty free. The problem was solved when they invited ten of the young people they had met to a soiree at their home that night. The condition was that we all had to take a bottle each in our handbags and as we were in transit the customs people weren't interested. A good night was had by all.

Before I left Europe I had written to the ABC in Melbourne telling them their best journalist was on his way home and asking 'How about a job?' On arrival in Hawaii I had some very good news; a telegram was waiting telling me I had my old job back. That was a good start. The ship was to leave at midnight, so I went to a bar nearby to use up the few remaining US dollars I had. I was accosted by a rather weepy woman who had flown from San Francisco to meet her husband who was on rest and recreation leave from the war in Vietnam. According to her story her husband was looking forward to his leave and meeting female company but his wife was not included in the list. I sympathised with her and earnt a drink for my efforts.

In 1966 Australia had turned to decimal currency and some of us returning from Europe on the *Orsova* still had some two-cent coins in our pockets. It didn't take us long to find out that in the ship's casino the sixpence sterling machines accepted the Australian two-cent pieces. The sixpenny machines were soon closed for the rest of the voyage after winners were rewarded with a pile of Australian two-cent coins. In Suva, the capital of Fiji, the *Orsova* was possibly the first of the big liners to visit the city. The ship was welcomed by a Fijian military band in full regalia and naturally, throngs of hopeful shopkeepers. In Auckland, New Zealand, a letter was waiting for me from the ABC with the official notification that my request for employment had been noted and was being considered. It was good to see the wheels of bureaucracy were still running smoothly.

The wonderful around-the-world journey ended as the *Orsova* sailed into Sydney harbour on Boxing Day 1968. Going through customs was interesting. I have already mentioned Australia's obsession with censorship, and drugs were not on the radar in those days. My vigilant customs officer chose to search the case which had all the little bits and pieces and souvenirs of the trip. Right along the bottom of the bag were 14 boxes of 35 mm colour slides I had had developed in London. Each article he pulled out was listed on my customs declaration until he arrived at the boxes at the bottom of the case. He looked at the boxes, then looked at me and asked in a very serious tone, 'Were there any photographs there you would not show your mother?' I thought to myself I had better keep a straight face or I could be here for a week going through each box which contained 36 slides. Looking very indignant I said, 'Certainly not!' That satisfied him. and I was free to go with the booklets I had got from the Netherlands, the ones I would not have shown my mother, hidden at the bottom of another small case. I stayed for a day with a friend in Sydney, and I had just enough money to pay for the trip to Melbourne on the Southern Aurora where I was met by my father who took me back to Gnarwarre.

NINE

Back to Work and Walking

The necessity now was to work hard, get some money together and of course pay off my mother's loan. With some overtime, many strange shifts, an occasional cash job as a waiter and a very cheap one-bedroom flat, I was able to accumulate enough money to buy a Renault 10 car. I am sure the salesman would not have guessed what area or type of country this car would eventually traverse. I was on the move again a year later in 1969. With a friend who liked hiking, I decided to walk to Mount Albert in the forest country east of Warburton. Having walked through most of the cities I visited in Europe I was in fairly good condition for this type of travel. We drove to Big River just east of Warburton, which is

Cliff's ABC profile photo, 1969

east of Melbourne. The car was left in a parking area from where we set off for what should have been a three-hour hike. Our bushwalking map showed us the path. We came to an intersection and mistakenly took the wrong path. Later we found it was a new path not shown on our map. The one we should have taken was slightly overgrown. We realised we were lost when the sun was in the wrong position if we were heading for our destination. Working on the lie of the land we eventually found Big River and we knew where our car was. At this point it was getting dark. We could see the road on the other side but it was too difficult to cross the river. Also it had begun to rain heavily so we made a mia mia, a less than waterproof structure of tree branches and ferns, and huddled together in front of a fire which helped a little bit when not rained upon. The next day two weary and wet walkers found a place to cross Big River and walk back to the Renault 10.

This experience did not deter us two months later from hiking from Neerim Junction to Warburton which took two days. We had camping gear this time. The local bus service that stopped at every farm gate to deliver mail eventually got us to our starting point. We followed old tramlines which had been used to haul timber from the forest to the nearest railway station. The hike was fairly easy going until we came to one point where the tramline came to the bottom of a cliff. The timber from the tramlines at the top of the cliff was then lowered by chains to the tram trucks waiting at the bottom to continue the journey. As this means of getting the timber hadn't been used since the 1930s, we had to carefully scramble up the cliff face, find the old tramlines and continue the trek. The other hazard was that a lot of the tram way used timber trestle bridges to cross streams and gullies. Many had not survived subsequent bushfires so that meant going down the banks, wading across streams and scrambling up the other side. No problem camping overnight as planned but we did enjoy a hot coffee, and the comfort of the train at Warburton which took us back to Melbourne. That railway is now closed.

The years 1969 and 1970 were years of working and consolidation, which meant only short trips exploring the Otway Ranges, Cape Otway and the Portland and Mount Gambier regions in the west of Victoria. The main reason for this careful harvesting of money was a large deposit I had placed on an apartment in the Melbourne suburb of Windsor. This did not stop a weekend camping trip with Rodney Smith, a name you will read again further on as we shared several long trips around Australia. We decided to spend a weekend camping in the Barmah Forest on the New South Wales side of the border near Echuca in Victoria. On the way there we bought some oranges in Echuca to take with us. In 1970 at many border crossings there was a Department of Agriculture officer to check if you were carrying fruit because of the problem of fruit fly. The following day on the return trip we were stopped at the border and were told to surrender the few remaining oranges we had. We told the officer we had actually bought the fruit in Echuca in Victoria but to no avail so we had a feast of oranges on the spot. A few weeks later Rodney and I were camping in the Wyperfield National Park in north-west Victoria. It was March and the weather was warm so we just slept in sleeping bags on the ground under a tarpaulin stretched from the Renault 10. No one told us there was a mouse plague in the district. We woke up early because of rustling noises to find both sleeping bags were covered with thousands of grey field mice. They covered the whole area so we rose quickly and tucked our trousers into our socks, a trick I had learnt while working on my father's farm. Having a mouse run up the inside of your trousers sounds funny but it is not. We shook out the sleeping bags and drove off to find a rodent-free place for breakfast.

My apartment was still being built and I wasn't due to move in until late 1971 so I used the time for short day or overnight trips to places around Melbourne I had not had the opportunity to visit before, or wanted to have a second look at. This also included a week driving to Sydney through Albury and Wagga Wagga and returning via the coast on a much improved Princes Highway. There were now new bridges replacing the old creek crossings.

I was still into hiking and in March 1971, six of us tried out a two-day hike through the Victorian Alpine Park to the remote but beautiful Lake Tali Karn. We decided to take one walking path in and a second path to return. We drove two cars to Tamboritha Road east of Licola, parked one at the start of the hike and the other at the end of the second track. The hike was great, crossing the Wellington River some 20 times as the first track followed the river, a small stream as it was at this stage in its life. We were happy to see the cars at the end of the second day. We were actually surprised to see several other groups at the camp site in such a remote place.

By May I was ready to make use of my annual leave which I had accumulated since returning from overseas. With Rodney Smith as my companion I decided to introduce the Renault 10 to the outback which meant equipping it with a crash bar to ward off kangaroos or any other livestock which might be in the wrong place at the wrong time. We headed north with no trouble through such delightfully named places as Coonabarabran in New South Wales, Bindle and Bogantungan in Central Queensland. We travelled west to Longreach where the true test for the Renault

10 came when we turned north to travel on what was claimed to be the Landsborough Highway. In actual fact in 1971 it was a black earth graded track that turns to grey dust in summer and is impassable after any decent rain. The dirt turns to mud which sticks to and accumulates on the tyres, bringing any vehicle to a halt. On this trip the road was rock hard but it had rained some days before and trucks battling the conditions had left deep ruts in the track. The Renault 10 managed to straddle these ruts except once when I got caught and slid along with all wheels in the ruts. This pushed a protective plate under the vehicle up against the gear shift mechanism resulting in a nerve-racking clanging sound every time I changed gear. In Mount Isa I took the car to the local Renault dealer whose only comment was, 'So that's what a Renault 10 looks like.' It appears small cars didn't often make it to Mount Isa. He said I should take it to a service station on the outskirts of the city as the bloke there had just come from Victoria and might

Landsborough Highway north of Winton, June 1971

be able to help. The Victorian service station proprietor said, 'No worries', put the car on a hoist, took off the bent protective plate, attacked the dents with a sledgehammer, screwed the plate back on and we were able to drive off clang-free.

From Camooweal west of 'the Isa' we turned north on again what was laughingly called the Gregory Highway, a graded dirt road that again would have been impassable in the wet. Driving on stretches of flat saltpans was no trouble. However the problems began with the stony, very rough, ridges which separated the flat sections. The engine of the Renault 10 is at the back and the drive shafts go independently to each rear wheel. This meant that on one or two occasions, with the protective plate again showing its value, I had one rear wheel losing traction as I was forced to drive over a large stone, while the other rear wheel was keeping the car moving. The large air cleaner over the top of the engine was held on a by a small nut which eventually gave way with this type of treatment. We made sure the air cleaner stayed put by using an old faithful of all travellers, the wire coat hanger. This proved very successful. At the end of the trip I saw my local dealer who suggested it be left on as it was better value than the small nut designed for smooth French highways.

We made Burketown by early afternoon and decided to fill up with petrol. At the service station I was asked how much petrol I needed. I consulted the gauge and said four gallons should do. With that the attendant hand-pumped four gallons into a glass measuring bowl at the top of the pump and drained the petrol into my tank. That's what happens when there are no electric pumps. Between Burketown and Normanton there was a creek crossing at a place called Floraville. Two concrete culverts were placed side by side crossing the waterway. I did not notice a four centimetres difference in height between the two slabs, and hit the sharp edge heavily, blowing the two front tyres. Fortunately we carried two spare tyres. The large trucks the crossing was designed for would not have been affected by the height difference. While Rodney and I were changing tyres a road train pulled up and the driver offered help. We thanked him and said we were OK. He then went through numerous gears and got the road train rolling again, presumably wondering what two idiots in a small car with Victorian number plates were doing around the edge of the Gulf of Carpentaria.

From Normanton we drove 70 kilometres to Karumba right on the Gulf, in time to see the prawn trawlers unloading their catch. Thousands of prawns were carried on conveyer belts from the trawlers to the processing plant. On each side of the road between Karumba and Normanton was tall tropical grass about two metres high so we did not see much of the countryside. It is a seasonal phenomenon. Going eastwards we travelled through the old gold-mining town of Croydon, at one stage a city of 20 000 people. We saw a few remaining houses, the railway station at the end of the line from Normanton and a two-storey wooden hotel standing guard over the rather desolate scene Then we continued to the Atherton tableland and down to Cairns.

After some rest and recreation in Cairns and trips to Green Island and Kuranda, we headed north again, on the road to Cooktown. The road then was a graded dirt and gravel road with no culverts over creeks and waterways; we counted 27 of them. The first stop was at Mount Molloy where we were told the local baker made pies to die for. The information was correct. On the way we also encountered bulldust, the real stuff, for the first time. This is caused by the constant pounding of vehicles over the fine gravel roads turning the surface into thin talcum-like dust over 30 centimetres deep in places. I was going too fast the first time I met it and immediately this huge dust cloud enveloped the car including the windscreen, cutting out all visibility.

In Cairns when we mentioned to someone we were going on to Cooktown we were told to look out for the Cooktown bus because it generally broke down during the journey. Sure enough we met the bus which had broken down. We asked the driver if he needed help but said he would be all right; he knew how to get the old bus going again. The passengers had taken the opportunity to get out of the bus and go for a stroll. These included a small group of middle-aged to elderly ladies. They appeared rather fascinated by the two young blokes wearing only very skimpy Speedos sitting in the car. They seemed very interested to hear our story. I might add the Speedos were ideal, not only for the climate, but also they saved time by not having to wash the dust out of shirts and trousers. The Renault 10 had very good air-conditioning – you opened all the windows and let the dust blow in and then hopefully out.

At Laura, the most northern section of the Cooktown road, we were talking to a local at the store who told us where we could see some little-known Aboriginal rock art, off the beaten track. We followed his directions and on a little-used track found the caves and cliff face with the rock drawings in very good condition. Since then I have heard they are now open to the public but well protected against vandalism. I also presume the track has been improved. On the return trip from Cooktown, in a bulldust section, we came across a Vanguard estate car, similar to the one I had owned, with its nose in a pile of bulldust and dirt. The driver apparently skidded after hitting the dust. He asked if we could tow him out. I told him my car was too small for that job but I did mention that as we left Cooktown we were followed by two trucks which should be able to help. He seemed quite happy about that and appeared fairly relaxed as he helped himself to another can of beer. There were several empty ones in the front of the car and a number of full ones on the back seat. He was certainly not going to die of thirst in the foreseeable future. I am not prepared to judge whether the beer played a part in his predicament.

Cooktown road Reedy St. George Creek crossing,
Palmer River, November 1971

We had a few days to do the tourist bit around Cairns before heading home. With our holiday leave running out we had a fairly straightforward trip home over a week, using the Pacific and Hume Highways without incident.

TEN

A Lifelong Travelling Partner

One way that I decided what place I would visit when I had a spare day or two was to take a large road map of Victoria, spread it on a table, shut my eyes, spin the map around and put my finger on it. The place where my finger landed was the place I would visit, going one way and returning by a different route. On the morning of Friday 1 October 1971 my finger landed on the town of Moulamein in southern New South Wales. My map did cover that area north of Swan Hill. That evening I joined some friends in the saloon bar at the Prince of Wales Hotel in St Kilda and met a young man called Rob Young. We got on well together and I ended up staying the night at his place.

Next morning I told him of my plans to drive to Moulamein about 400 kilometres away and asked if he wanted to come. Surprisingly he said yes and so I had a companion. We spent the second night together in Moulamein and the third night at my place and we have been together ever since. You will read his name many times from now on as we both share a love of travel. (After the change in marriage laws in 2017, we were married in February 2018.) The trip to Moulamein was interesting. We got to know each other better, which says something about sitting in a small car together for 10 hours, but as far as the reader is concerned nothing happened to write home about.

The next year, 1972, we had moved into my new flat in Windsor and had combined our holidays planning a trip to Adelaide. On the day we were to depart, the full effects of a petrol strike was being felt and we were warned we that may not find petrol in South Australia. Undeterred, we headed to north Sydney and then on to the Gold Coast having been assured there was still some petrol available on the way. However by the time we reached Sydney the situation was worse so we left the car with friends in Parramatta, got the train to Murwillumbah and then the bus across the border to Coolangatta. We returned the same way to Sydney. By this time petrol was again flowing so we headed west through the Blue Mountains, visited the Jenolan Caves and continued west. The Renault 10 performed magnificently, handling the winding roads without effort, and the air cleaner was still attached with the coat hanger.

It was July and at Orange we discovered on the next morning why the hotel we were in felt cold — the Renault was covered in snow but being of French descent it carried on and safely got us back to Melbourne via Parkes and south through Griffith and Shepparton. When I returned to work, at the time at television station Channel O (now Channel 10), there had been a change in management policy and I no longer had a job. After some negotiations, assisted by my union, the Australian Journalists' Association, I had some money and a bit of free time. I put off looking for employment and decided to make use of the itinerary we had planned for the visit to South Australia. In two days I reached Broken Hill with an overnight stop at Ouyen. Instead of taking the Barrier Highway to South Australia I decided to return to the highway after visiting the old mining town of Silverton. On the map the road from Broken Hill to Silverton was well defined, then there was a dotted line showing a road or track going west to the Barrier Highway. I followed the map and took a dirt track as directed which led me to the front yard of a farmhouse. I showed the farmer my map and he said that there had been a track at some time but recommended I didn't try it as he even had trouble getting cattle along it. I took his advice, retreated to Broken Hill and sped along the Barrier Highway as far as Yunta. There I headed north west to reach Hawker in the centre of the Flinders Ranges.

My small car seemed to take corrugations in its stride. I had very little use for the crash bar on its front except once a passing truck threw up a sizeable stone which hit the top of the crash bar with a loud clang and then ricocheted off it, spinning over the top of the car. One windscreen saved!

I headed south from Hawker beside the remains of the old Ghan railway line, arriving at Port Augusta. This was followed by a lap around the Yorke Peninsula. Travelling on a dirt track alongside a beach in the Innes National Park I came across the remains of an old shipwreck with its rusting frame stranded on the sand. I ended up in Adelaide after tasting the Barossa Valley, then headed back to Melbourne to look for work. On the way back I saw the giant lobster at Kingston South East. These giant models appear in a number of towns highlighting local industries or historic moments. Koalas, bananas and Ned Kelly come to mind.

The next year, 1973, was spent making short trips over weekends. I had managed to get my job back at the ABC for the third time, and annual leave had to be earnt. However one weekend we did take one of the last Sunday excursion trains from Geelong to Queenscliff run by the Victorian Railways. The line is now closed, although volunteers of the Bellarine Tourist Railway operate a section from Drysdale to Queenscliff. From Melbourne the train of ten wooden carriages was pulled by a regular diesel locomotive. At Geelong a small lightweight 'T' class diesel took over. Its main job was shunting trucks around in goods yards and despite only a handful of passengers it did make very hard work of a fairly steep climb from Moolap up to Leopold, I presume in bottom gear. After that it was all downhill to Queenscliff at the entrance to Port Philip Bay. The line was closed a few weeks later.

After a year of hard work (my appraisal) I had earnt my annual leave. My old travelling companion, Rodney Smith, who was also working at the ABC at the time wanted to visit Central and Northern Australia and invited me and another of his friends, Carl Schulz. Unfortunately, Rob had to stay at home and earn a living. Rodney had a 1958 Holden sedan that he kept in immaculate condition but had no hesitation taking it anywhere he wanted to go, no matter how rough or dirty the track was. It was also large enough to take three men and their camping gear comfortably. The idea was to camp out, which I was happy with. Carl's hobby and to some extent a sideline business was collecting and working on gems turning them into jewellery.

Our first destination was the Flinders Ranges in South Australia. We camped in Wilpena Pound. We climbed to the top of Saint Mary Peak, which gave us a great view of the area. The Pound is a flat plain surrounded by the ranges and at one stage was a cattle station. It is now a national park. We travelled south to Port Augusta before heading north on the Sturt Highway, which at that time was a gravel road.

With Carl on board and his interest in opals, our first stop was the mining town of Cooper Pedy. From afar there is very little to see of the town except the large hotel and several other buildings above ground, and of course the mounds from mine diggings. When you get there you find half the town is underground including a chapel and some shops. The below-ground living is a cool protection against the searing heat, especially in summer. The surface is bare gravel or stone with little or no vegetation. Through Carl's connections in the opal industry we were invited into one of the underground homes. There was little difference to the comforts of an above-ground home, with all the usual appliances, lounge chairs and carpets on the earthen floor. The owner told us of one problem. There were small shafts from the ceiling to the open air for ventilation. Occasionally a black snake, common in the area, found its way into these small shafts, ending up on the carpet. The locals were unfazed.

We left Cooper Pedy with Carl happily clutching a bag of raw opals he intended turning into fashionable gems. We took a north-west route mainly through station properties to reach Uluru (Ayers Rock as it was then). In the two days there we climbed the Rock and Rodney, being a bit of an exhibitionist, posed naked on the marker on its top. I have often wondered about the thoughts of two Japanese tourists who came over a small rise and saw this spectacle. Was it a local ritual and were they expected to do the same thing? One never knows. I might add the sensitivities of the local first Australians were not considered at that time. I can also appreciate why Uluru is an important part of local life with pools of water around the rock practically all the time because of occasional rain and overnight precipitation of dew.

The following day we drove to Kata Gina (then known as the Olgas), a group of rocks carved into valleys and peaks by thousands of years of water and wind. With its gullies and springs

I found this more interesting and mysterious than the rock at Uluru. We were fortunate to run into a park ranger who explained the significance of its features and pointed out two ceremonial stone rings which had been used recently by the local people. The drive to Alice Springs was along a gravel road at that time. The two-day stop at 'the Alice' included trips to the gorges nearby, not to mention more practical things like visiting the laundromat.

Once again we headed north, this time on the bitumen Sturt Highway, getting a taste of the north in more ways than one in the hotels at Tennant Creek and Katherine, and including a swim in the mineral springs pool at Mataranka of outback literary fame. In Darwin I chose the luxury of a hotel bed leaving the tent to my two mates. Relaxed and refreshed we piled into the Holden and headed towards Mount Isa, going the back way through Cape Crawford which, despite the name, is nowhere near the sea. We also learnt the value of carrying extra fuel as several stations we passed had large signs on their gates saying they had no fuel for sale. To get fuel to the stations was a costly business and they weren't prepared to sell it to tourists who had not planned in advance.

We found Mount Isa was not a particularly friendly place for visitors. The inhabitants were making money working on the mines and they had little time for much else except, it appears, gambling, which despite the protest of the politicians and the studied ignorance of the police was readily available, and mostly illegal. Heading south towards Longreach, just past Boulia we stopped at the Hamilton Creek Hotel. There is no other building in the settlement and the creek itself is a dry river bed which may see water occasionally in the wet season. Despite the isolation there were several vehicles including a truck parked outside the hotel. While we were there every vehicle on the road stopped at the hotel, not that there were very many travelling that day. We met the driver of the truck at the bar looking the worse for wear. He told us his sad story. His truck had broken down, and it was going to take three to four days for a part to arrive from Brisbane via Longreach. He had another one or two days waiting for the part and with nothing to do at Hamilton Creek it was becoming a long, hard wait propped at the bar. Not long after enjoying our first drink the proprietor, tongue in cheek, introduced the bar to the Hamilton Creek tug-o'-war team. This consisted of his wife who was, in contrast to our host who was short and slim, to put it politely, of broad and tall stature, followed by the two daughters who were of the same imposing nature. I imagine quite a formidable team at any time.

From Longreach we travelled south through Charleville, my old stamping ground with no sign of change in the 13 years since I was last there. At Wyandra the lady at the general store did remember my name from the time I worked at 4VL Charleville. That gave me a bit of a buzz. Going south we passed through Cunnamulla heading for Bourke, stopping briefly at the North Bourke hotel which is on the west side of the Darling River, and has a historical reputation from the droving days when the cattle came to Bourke to be loaded onto rail trucks for sale in Sydney. The Dubbo to Bourke railway line is now closed as road transport has replaced the rail. At least we had been 'to the back of Bourke'. With annual leave time running out we arrived back in Melbourne three days later, thankfully not delayed by some flooding between Forbes and Narrandera.

The annual leave for 1975, I decided, would be used for a drive around Tasmania as I hadn't had a chance to see a lot of the state since hitchhiking around it 23 years previously. Rob was also able to get some leave, not as generous as mine, and we arranged for him to meet me in Hobart when I got there. I hired a car for the drive and it was waiting for me at Launceston airport; a fire-engine red Holden Torana. At least I would have no difficulty finding it in a parking lot. I quickly learnt that there were no such things as long straight stretches of road in Tasmania, and luckily I had planned a leisurely drive.

From Launceston I headed west, more or less following the coast, passing through the succession of small towns and villages that line Bass Strait. From Wynyard I turned south to go through what I had been told was the wild west of the state. Halfway is the old tin- mining settlement of Waratah where I chose to stay the night. The first thing I noticed was the huge old tin-mining dredge, too big to move after the mine closed, and slowly rusting away at the point it last loaded the ore. Then I saw Bischoff's Hotel, a white two-storey wooden building that probably arrived at the same time as the miners. At the bar I asked for a room for the night and was immediately asked if I played snooker. I replied, 'Sort of', which was good enough. I then had my name put down for the hotel's annual snooker tournament before being shown my room. I still wonder if I had said 'No', would I have got a room? A sweet mystery of life. For the record I was beaten in the first round but I can skite it was by the young man who went on to win the tournament.

Next day I had a stop at Zeehan, which at one time was an important town in the mining industry in its heyday and centre of a rail system that serviced the mines. I spent some time at the museum admiring the old steam engines that were preserved. A railway line then connected Zeehan to Burnie, the nearest port. I wound my 'fire-engine' Toyota on through to Strahan and across the range into Queenstown, seeing for the first time the barren hills around the town where the vegetation had been killed by the fumes from the big zinc mine. I made sure I visited the Australian Rules football ground, a reddish-brown oval of gravel with not a blade of grass in sight. A local told me Queenstown had never lost a match on its home ground. I can certainly understand why.

Winding my way to Hobart, taking two days to get there, around Cradle Mountain, Bronte and Tarraleah, I saw the results of the Hydro Electricity Commission power stations and dams that were being built when I got lifts from the HEC trucks while hitchhiking in 1952. Rob duly arrived in Hobart as planned and after a look at the city we then headed for the old convict prison of Port Arthur. On the way, at Richmond, we took a break and I had a good laugh as Rob began feeding some ducks near the historic bridge. Being well tourist orientated, they arrived en masse at the first chance of a free feed. He eventually extricated himself from

Rob with ducks Richmond, September 1975

101

their enthusiastic advances. The ruins at Port Arthur impressed us but you did grieve for the poor souls who built them, and where they were imprisoned, not to mention the trivial crimes for which they were convicted. As planned we returned to Hobart and zig-zagged up the east coast and ended up in Launceston to return the 'red devil', as we called the Holden, to Budget Rent-a-car, and flew home.

ELEVEN

South East Asia Beckons

With just a few days left in 1975 we began Rob's first visit overseas, a trip through Singapore, Malaysia and Indonesia. The first surprise for me was as we were approaching Singapore a hostess invited us into the cockpit of the Qantas Boeing 727. We were given seats behind the pilots as we landed in Singapore. It was a fascinating experience watching the plane approach the runway lit up at night and observing the drill the pilots went through as we landed. Security wasn't as rigid then. Rob had arranged this by giving a letter to the chief steward when we boarded the plane giving details of who we were and our backgrounds, and requesting the visit. It worked well.

As we boarded the train to Kuala Lumpur we passed through Malaysian customs. Having experienced border crossings in Europe I was wearing tailored trousers and shirt. I forgot to warn Rob about the dress code at borders and he presented himself in a rather sloppy pair of shorts and a well-worn soft shirt. I passed through quickly and then waited patiently as he assured the officials that he did have a return ticket, a hotel booking and some money. On board the train he said he would improve his standard of dress at every future border crossing. The train journey gave us glimpses of the local agriculture and introduced us to the local tropical fruit, rambutan, a bit messy but delicious. These were sold by young women walking through the carriages with baskets of the fruit and other edibles.

On New Year's Day, 1976, we boarded a very long train to Butterworth along with what seemed to be several thousand other would-be passengers. As the train slowly came into the station with its doors open we took the advice from a local traveller, and when it slowed down enough grabbed the pole beside the door with one hand, suitcase in the other and swung ourselves on board and made for a good window seat. We just did as the locals did. Halfway through the journey the train wound its way through the central mountain range of Malaysia where there had been trouble with some communist terrorists. As we went through the area, concerned armed soldiers walked through the carriage, and as the train crossed bridges and causeways there were guards on both sides of the structures.

We arrived safely in Butterworth and got a ferry across to Georgetown on the island of Penang where we had booked our hotel. During our stay in Georgetown, after sight-seeing during the day, we had arranged to meet a friend of ours that night staying at a resort at Batu Feringgi on the coast, some 10 kilometres of winding road from Georgetown. We used the local bus to get there. After a pleasant evening we got the last bus back, experiencing the fastest ride I can remember on public transport. The driver was obviously very anxious to finish work. We clung to our seats as the almost empty 40-seat bus swayed around corners, went flat out on the straight sections and braked viciously around the next corner, all in the dark. Not for the same reasons, we were as pleased as the driver when we reached the terminus, and we were just as pleased as he was to leave the bus.

Our flight from Georgetown to Medan in north-east Sumatra consisted of the Malaysia Air plane taking off, doing a right turn and landing at Medan in around about 20 minutes. The Indonesian customs officer was concerned that we were bringing in a set of pewter goblets made from Malaysian tin. Being pre-warned about importing these items we weren't surprised at his interest. However we had declared them as imports. The customs officer wanted to keep them and said we would get them back when we left Denpasar airport in Bali some two weeks later and some 1000 kilometres away. I put the chances of that happening as the same as winning the big lottery prize. I pointed out that we would keep the mugs and I had the address and telephone number of the Australian Consulate in Medan which we would contact if there was a problem. With us refusing to offer a little financial help to sort out the situation, the said mugs were thrust back in the bag and we entered Indonesia. Incidentally this time both of us were conservatively dressed as we passed through customs. Not knowing where our hotel was we hired a taxi which drove us out of the airport, did a left-hand turn, and drove us into the hotel right next door. Them's the breaks.

The next stage of our tour took us to the village of Tuk Tuk on Samosir Island in Lake Toba which is actually the crater of a huge volcano. After sorting out our tickets and getting two seats on a hopelessly overbooked bus, we started our journey. The problem with seats on local buses in Indonesia was that they were designed for slightly thinner Asian bodies, not two well-fed Australians, so we took it in turns half-standing to relieve the pressure on our backsides. The luggage of all passengers was strapped onto the roof of the bus, so we kept an eye on what luggage was coming off the roof at each stop. Our destination was Parapat from where we got a boat to Tuk Tuk. The bus broke down (within sight of Parapat, thankfully) and we waited patiently beside the road as repairs were carried out and we eventually arrived at our stop. At Tuk Tuk we learnt a lesson we remembered on many later travels. The local Bintang beer, a very nice drop, was a quarter of the price at the village store as against what was being charged at the tourist hotel.

The bus trip from Medan partly prepared us for the next leg of the journey, an 18-hour bus trip from Parapat to Bukit Tinggi in central Sumatra. Again the bus was overbooked and to solve the problem several wooden chairs were taken from a local café and placed in the aisle. As we wound our way through the jungle we came to a halt because of a truck broken down in the centre of the road. At that point the camber of the road sloped into the centre so the truck tilted to the centre. Our bus tried to squeeze past but it also sloped into the centre. The driver and some passengers got out and placed stones in the centre of the road so that eventually our bus was straightened enough to scrape past the truck, and I literally mean 'scraped past'. I noticed that the other truck drivers stayed in their vehicles and Indonesian bus passengers also stayed in their seats. Later I found out that this was tiger country and a tiger attack was not unknown.

As evening closed in we stopped at a wayside roadhouse for a meal and a toilet break. There were no toilets on the bus. For the men the toilet was a path that led to an outdoor area where you had to cater for your own needs. Very basic is a good description. For a meal there were various bowls of cold cooked meats and local vegetables, none of which I could recognise but we ate it regardless. I'm not sure what the meat dish I had was, but judging by the shape of the bone it was either dog or monkey, but I'm still here to tell the tale.

The next stage of the journey was the very steep descent from the mountain plateau to the coastal plain. As the bus entered the first of a series of tunnels the driver's assistant took a torch to check if the luggage piled on top of the bus fitted under the tunnel roof. The driver then turned off the engine and gave several long blasts on the horn. As there was no sound from any other vehicle, we then started the drive down. After we came out of the first tunnel I looked down through the bus window to see the lights of a village practically directly some distance below in a valley, giving the impression of a sheer drop from the road. On reflection I'm glad we travelled at night. Perhaps I would not have been so relaxed if I could really see what was happening. Every time we entered a tunnel the bus kept in the centre of the road because of our luggage on the roof. At Bukit Tinggi we took a deep breath and relaxed.

Taking a deep breath was not recommended when I visited the local meat market. This was held under a large shed open on all sides. The range of slaughtered animals offered was wide and varied. The meat appeared fresh but the different aromas combined to make it quite breathtaking, and despite the large quantity of meat for sale there were no flies. Perhaps the climate was too hot. A small river ran through the city with steep cliffs on either side as the water, over the centuries, had formed a canyon through the volcanic ash of past eruptions. The solid river bed was being used as a vehicle wash for trucks.

We travelled by bus to nearby Padang to fly to Jakarta in Java. At the airport, while waiting for our cases, we chatted to a local man who had spent some time in Australia as a Colombo Plan student. We took his advice on the cost of getting a taxi from the airport to our hotel. He said 1500 rupee was a generous fare. We soon learnt the art of Asian bargaining. As we left the terminal the first quote we got was 5000 rupee. We explained in Indonesian – the little we had picked up – that that was too much. The next offer was 2500 rupee, a 50 per cent drop in the quote within 30 metres of walking, so we walked purposefully on. As we started walking from the terminal, a driver approached us and said he had a metered cab. In many parts of Asia there are metered taxis, but they are always broken when a Caucasian tourist looks like being a passenger. Our taxi driver took us to the hotel and we had 1200 rupee on his working meter. He received 1500 rupee for his troubles.

We used buses on our touring through western Java, and changed to a train to travel from Jogjakarta to Surabaya. We weren't particularly surprised when it arrived six hours late. By now we had become accustomed to Indonesia's leisurely approach to timetables. This meant some of the journey was done in the dark. As the sun goes down, night literally falls in the tropics. There is no twilight. For the past few days there had been heavy rains in the east of Java. As we approached a bridge we could hear the sounds of rushing water, and felt the cold air associated with large amounts of moving water. Through the train window we could see we were on a large, long bridge with the rushing river right up to the rails on the line. On each section of the bridge there was a man with a signal lamp telling the driver it was all right to proceed. The next day in Surabaya I read in an English language newspaper that, due to the floods, the railway line had been closed overnight. We could have been the last train to get through.

The next day on a tour of the city, I ended up at the waterfront. It was 1976 and a few days earlier, Indonesia had invaded the then Portuguese colony of East Timor. As I watched several large, heavily armed Indonesian naval ships left the area. An American tourist next to me got his camera out to photograph the ships. I moved hastily away, telling him there was a war on and to get back on board the cruise liner he was from, and take his photographs of the Indonesian navy in action from the safety of the liner's deck. He looked a bit startled and alarmed but did as I suggested. The bus from Surabaya to Denpasar on Bali took us as far as Banyuwangi where the bus with the passengers on board drove onto a ferry. With the front wheels on the ferry and the rear wheels still ashore, the ferry listed and the side of the ramp ruptured the diesel tanks on the bus. The bus was stranded half-on and half-off the ferry with diesel fuel spreading from the tank with locals, some smoking cigarettes, looking at the damage and wondering what to do next. Fearing that we may be incinerated because there was no way we could get off the bus, we yelled at the people to put out their cigarettes. Eventually the battered bus was able to reverse off the ferry and limp to a nearby garage where we waited for a replacement. The replacement bus duly arrived an hour or two later. Having survived one threat of immolation we were not impressed when those in charge would not let the passengers walk on board the ferry while the bus was driven on. The second time around we ended up safely on board.

On arrival at Denpasar we had another interesting tussle with local transport. We were booked in at the Legion Beach hotel at Kuta, a short distance from the Denpasar bus terminal. To get there we got a quote of 900 rupees from the driver of a bajai (a small utility with a covered tray for passengers behind the driver). By this time our Indonesian was basic but understandable and we told the driver the destination and checked the price in Indonesian. He assured us he knew where to go and so we set off with us and our luggage in the back of his bajai. It soon became evident he did not know where the hotel was and stopped at what looked like a backpacker hostel well away from the beach and the hotel. He said we had to get out there and pay him his money. We said we would not get out and we were prepared to sleep in the bajai until daylight when he could find his way to the Legion Beach Hotel. With that we both stretched out in the bajai and looked quite prepared to do as we said. He then started to drive off in what he thought was vaguely the right direction. He stopped a motorcyclist who then led him straight to the hotel. We paid the driver, collected our gear and left the motorcyclist and the driver arguing, as the motorcyclist wanted 600 rupee for showing the driver the way. The driver demanded we pay the motorcyclist. We refused, and the hotel staff came to collect us and our luggage. They told us not to worry as this drama apparently was often played out when guests arrived.

The week's break at the hotel was very welcome after three weeks of continuous travelling, even more so when I met Maria, a local lady who sold me ice-cold Bintang beer on the beach after my morning swim. Her price was 250 rupees, the price in the hotel bar 20 metres away was 600 rupees. One morning I forgot to bring any money. She told me not to worry, she would be there next morning, and I could pay her then. Next morning she was there and I did remember to bring the cash. Other beach sellers offered a range of wares including 'magic mushrooms' and sex with any gender I preferred, and in one case a 'friendly' goat. Also at night another sensory pleasure was available. As you walked along the beach at sunset the smell of marijuana smoke drifted from the sand dunes as people puffed and watched the sun sink in the west.

One request I did avoid came from the driver of our hire car, which took us on a day tour visiting the Kintamani volcano in the centre of Bali. The driver wondered if I would be good enough to take a small parcel back to a friend of his in Australia. I said I would be delighted but would have to declare it to Australian customs as it was not my property. End of conversation!

The return trip, flying from Denpasar to Sydney, was on a Garuda Airlines DC8. We noticed bolts or rivets turning on the wings. To us it was a bit unnerving, but we were assured by another passenger, who claimed to be a retired pilot, not to worry. In this type of aircraft you start to worry when they don't appear loose.

On our return to everyday existence we farewelled the Renault 10 and replaced it with a Renault 12 without the crash bar. Its first major run was along the Great Ocean Road to Warrnambool and a visit to nearby Tower Hill. Rob discovered that the emus in the reserve were large, had no fear of humans and expected all visitors to feed them. Rob escaped unscathed and the emu concerned went hungry.

In July I took part in a special celebration organised by Victorian Railways to commemorate the centenary of opening the line from Echuca to Deniliquin. Two special trains were involved, including one hauled by a steam engine. The usual speeches were made, the official dinner was provided by the town council, and everyone was told how great it was to have the railway operating. A month later the rail passenger service was replaced by a bus.

In October a friend joined us to take advantage of an offer by Ansett Airlines of a weekend flight from Melbourne to King Island in Bass Strait which included accommodation and the use of a car. The weekend went well, and the car was a 1939 Chevrolet, old, comfortable and reliable. On the Sunday morning we were told to go to the wharf where we could buy fresh crayfish caught that morning. This apparently was a common practice because, at the wharf, bags approved by Ansett were available to transport the live crayfish back to Melbourne. We landed in Melbourne, our small Fokker Friendship took its turn landing, squeezed in between the 747s from lands far away. We sensed a hint of envy as an announcement was made at the baggage collection for passengers from King Island to come to door four and collect their crayfish.

For the second year in succession we welcomed the new year in a foreign country. In 1977 it was New Zealand. Rob had annual leave due for January. He had not visited New Zealand and I had only briefly stepped ashore nine years earlier. We arranged to hire cars to drive through both the North and South Islands.

New Zealand has wonderful, breathtaking scenery, but the most breathtaking was landing at Wellington Airport. It's not so much the scenery but the actual landing. The runway goes across a narrow strip of land between two hills. As we approached all I could see was water as we got lower and lower, and then I felt the wheels touch the runway. At the end of the runway as we turned to go to the arrival area, again all I could see was water, this time at the other end of the runway. From then on the tour of the North Island went like clockwork. The car was ready for us, all hotel bookings were as planned, the road maps were correct, the car ran beautifully and the locals were friendly. We admired the scenery, and, like Tasmania, we found straight stretches of road were few and far between.

We saw 1977 in at Rotorua amid the geysers and the bubbling mud pools. A few days later on the road from Auckland to Hicks Bay we stopped at Whakatane to watch Wakaari in the Bay of Plenty erupting. Even at quite a distance, it looked spectacular. From Point Hicks we made our way, at a leisurely rate, along the east coast to Wellington from where we flew to Christchurch to pick up our second hire car. We made our way south to Invercargill and to Bluff, the most southern point of New Zealand's South Island. In the North Island we reached Cape Reinga, the most northern point. On leaving Invercargill a policeman pulled Rob over for exceeding the speed limit, by only a few knots I might add. On seeing Rob's Victorian licence he decided the paperwork wasn't worth the trouble. By the time the summons appeared, we would be out of the country.

We drove to Milford Sound and I found driving through the tunnel under Mount Christina was very deceptive. There was no indication I was making a fairly steep descent until I felt the car getting away from me. Coming the other way, it was a case of using the lower gears as you drove up the reverse incline. Breathtaking is the right way to describe the Sound. We took a short flight over the area and the pilot was a bit grim-faced on landing when a wind gust blew us off the runway into the gravel.

The next scenic flight was even more lip-biting. From Milford Sound we visited Queenstown before driving to Mount Cook National Park staying at the Hermitage hotel. The day we drove into the Park, the sky was clear and Mount Cook rose majestically above the other mountains so we booked a scenic flight for the next day. The conditions looked good as we took off and started flying above the Tasman Glacier. The idea was to land on the glacier before resuming the flight. As we approached the northern end of the glacier a thick cloud enveloped the plane with visibility limited to only a few metres. The pilot said we had a problem, and he warned we may get quite close to the cliff face so he could get his bearings to try to fly down the valley to get under the cloud bank. After a few minutes of blind flying with all of us holding our breaths and hoping, we burst out of the cloud into brilliant sunshine. As we headed for the Mount Cook airport we found the runway occupied by the scheduled service flight from Christchurch so we got an unplanned flight over Lake Pukaki.

Rob beside glacier-landing plane at Mount Cook, New Zealand, January 1977

From Mount Cook we crossed the alps, staying at Haast on the west coast of the South Island. The next day we headed north in pouring rain bound for Greymouth. On the way we made our way up a rough and narrow road to view the Franz Joseph Glacier. On reading the fine print on our hire car contract we found out later that we should not have taken the car on that particular road. One lesson: never read the fine print. It's always your fault if anything happens. Check airline and cruise ship tickets! The rain kept tumbling down all the way to Greymouth where a local told us that this happened for three hundred days of the year. We put our little hire car, a small Datsun, to the test as we wound our way through the northern hills of the South Island, admiring the scenery or staring fixedly at the narrow, winding gravel roads, depending on who was driving. Eventually we delivered the car in one piece at the Christchurch airport and flew back to Melbourne.

TWELVE

From Four Wheels to Two

Living in Windsor and working in Elsternwick meant that the distance was too short to warrant driving. There was no direct public transport and walking, especially after a trying day in the office, was not my favourite option. At the age of 41, I decided to buy a bicycle and cycle to work. It was a great decision. It meant I took only 15 to 20 minutes to get to work, no matter what the weather or traffic was like. The exercise also made me fitter. I started to take short rides around the suburbs on some of the days I had off and I enjoyed it. I then decided to try a longer trip doing a six-day ride from Albury to Swan Hill. I chose this route because I worked out that by following the Murray River downstream I would be riding downhill more or less all the way.

I prepared the bicycle with two panniers attached to a carrier rack over the rear wheel and a basket in front of the handlebars. The panniers carried clothes and the two spare tyre tubes while the front basket had the repair kit, maps and wallet. Two water bottles were fitted to the main frame. I planned to ride about 100 to 120 kms a day, with an average speed of 15 kph. I did not carry camping gear, deciding that after riding a bicycle during the day a comfortable motel bed was what I deserved at night. After all,

I was over 40 and sort of feeling my age; anyhow, that was my excuse. Where I could, I picked quiet back roads to ride along, enjoying the fresh air, the quietness, the scenery and animal life, not being disturbed by noisy vehicles. Occasionally I would also get a wave from a farmer working near the road. It was a great feeling, and I was hooked. On the downside I soon realised that my backside also had to get into training to cope with sitting on a bicycle seat for long periods. It took several days before I didn't have to gently lower my tender rear portion onto the seat.

One overnight stop was at Torrumbarry, a small settlement on the Murray at the weir of the same name. It was a hot day as I rode up to the hotel, which had a glass front facing the highway. I leant the bicycle against the glass and walked into the bar intending to ask for a room for the night. As I walked in, and before I could say anything, the barman handed me a pot of cold beer and said 'You'll need this!' He was right and, better still, that first one turned out to be on the house. There was a motel room available and so I had a good meal and a good sleep.

The next night I was not so lucky. I rode from Torrumbarry along the River Track, a narrow dirt track following the river through the Gunbower Forest. The track was quite good except there were pools of water that were fine to ride through but I disturbed swarms of mosquitoes and I was very glad I carried the tropical-strength insect repellent. My destination for the night was Murrabit, at one time the terminus of a railway branch line. Because of this I assumed there would be a hotel. There had been but it had burnt down quite some time ago and had not been rebuilt. I went to the general store and asked if there was a bed and breakfast place or if someone had a caravan I could hire for the night. I was told to see a lady just around the corner where

Cliff with loaded bicycle ready for travel, September 1977

there was a caravan parked in front of the house. The owner was quite happy for me to use it for the night. We negotiated a price and I was directed to the nearby park where there was a toilet and washbasin. Praise to the local council because the toilet block was clean and well cared for. The caravan was also quite comfortable and I was able to get food from the general store. The following day the tracks through the forest along the banks of the Murray took me to my destination, Swan Hill. Booking in at a motel the young receptionist asked me for my vehicle registration number. She appeared a little apprehensive when I said my vehicle was not registered and then I pointed to the bicycle in view from the reception desk. A good night's sleep and the morning train to Melbourne completed my first long-distance bicycle trip but definitely not the last. After that trip, riding the bicycle to work was much more comfortable – the backside had adapted to a new working environment.

After seven years together, Rob had come to share my appreciation of good wine. In 1978 with some leave due we loaded up the Renault 12 and aimed first for the Flinders Ranges in South Australia which I had been praising since my first visit and then the wine areas of the Barossa and McLaren Vale. We had a variety

Murray River track, Gunbower Forest, May 1977

of scenery to view as we made our way over several days through north- west Victoria, the South Australian Riverland area, the old mining town of Burra, and the Clare Valley before arriving at the motel at Wilpena Pound in the Flinders Ranges National Park. A scenic flight over the range revealed to us the size and extent of the dry salt lake beds that disappear in the desert to the west. On maps these are named as lakes with dotted lines outlining their size. Apart from a rare wet season they are in actual fact beds of dry salt formed by thousands of years of an occasional flood and continuous evaporation. The flight gave us a glimpse of the emptiness and vastness of the outback.

On the ground we severely tested the Renault 12's suspension on the roads leading to the mining town of Leigh Creek. On some sections the 'gravel' is larger rocks of sharp quartz forming the road, probably good enough for trucks with tractor-treaded tyres but the road managed to shred one of our city-bred tyres. Luckily the service station at Blinman had a tyre that fitted, and the price, as expected, was not a cut-price special. With all tyres intact we returned from Leigh Creek, staying overnight at the old stone hotel at Parachilna, once a station on the original Ghan railway to Alice Springs, on the western side of the Flinders Ranges. The hotel was basic, food good, the bed comfortable and we did notice the hard earthen floor in our room. Very sensible when considering the dry and dusty conditions outside.

From Port Augusta we had a brief look at some of the natural gorges in the southern section of the Flinders Ranges before doing a tour of the Yorke Peninsula. We then headed east to the wineries in the Barossa Valley, and repeated the performance in the McLaren Vale region. We bought wines that we enjoyed tasting and had them freighted back to Rob's parents' home in the

Melbourne suburb of Elwood. We took the coastal route home once again seeing the giant lobster at Kingston South East and had a two-day stop at Nelson on the Victorian–South Australian border visiting the Princess Margaret Caves in the Lower Glenelg National Park. The caves were often not included in tourist itineraries but we felt it worth the visit. Arriving home we were met by Rob's somewhat irate parents demanding we remove 27 cases of wine that, for want of space, had been stacked in the living room. We hadn't really been keeping count of what we had bought so it was a bit of a surprise, reinforced when the credit card account arrived.

Later that year we took part in the 'Winery Walkabout' weekend arranged by the wineries around Rutherglen. On the Saturday night there was a big 'Walkabout' dinner in Wangaratta. We had booked in at a motel near the dinner venue which was a very wise move. We were served excellent food, copious quantities of wine with each course, and entertained by the Bushwackers, whose repertoire included much Australian country music with a touch of Irish. Rob left with the key to the motel room while I finished another very good glass of muscat. Shortly after I arrived back to the motel to find the door locked and no reaction to my knocking. Looking through the keyhole I saw that a fully-dressed Rob was sound asleep sprawled across the bed. At half-past one in the morning I decided it was not a good idea to wake the proprietor. I found I had the car keys in my pocket so, not feeling too much pain, curled up in its back seat. It was July and in Wangaratta at that time of the year the temperature can get below freezing point. That night it did. I could tell by my cold feet and the ice on the windscreen. From that day on we always got two keys for our motel room if they were available. If not, we both had car keys, so if we went different ways we locked the motel key in the boot of the car to be retrieved by the first one back. The plan works well as long as the first one back stays awake!

One clear result from our tour of the South Australian wineries and the trip to Rutherglen was that the two-bedroom flat in Windsor was overstocked with wine. We set off house hunting, looking for a house with an underground cellar to store wine. The imagination of real estate agents is boundless. One thought there was an old air-raid shelter somewhere in the front of one house but didn't know where the entrance was. Another showed us a small trapdoor in the kitchen under which we could store 12 bottles. Eventually Rob, without the help of any agents, found a house in East Hawthorn, nine kilometres from the central business district. It had no cellar but plenty of room. We eventually built our own air-conditioned room to store our wine collection. Now with a little more room for our collective hobby, the following year we organised a tour around the wine regions of central and northern Victoria, visiting many small towns in out-of-the-way places in the state.

It wasn't long before the urge to hop on the bicycle and pedal to more places took over. Being exposed to the elements, picking the time of the year was important – certainly not in the middle of summer or winter. I chose October for this pedal, aiming for Adelaide. The Vinelander train, now deceased, took my bicycle and its rider overnight from Melbourne for the launching of a ride from Mildura. The first two days' ride to Renmark in South Australia along the road beside the old railway branch line to Meringur was flat and easy going with plenty of mulga scrub to look at. On the third day I set off west from Renmark to Morgan pedalling into a 40-knot head wind. It was heavy going and by two thirds of the way I had run out of water. Then I noticed a windmill filling a sheep trough in a paddock beside the road, and worked out that the water should be all right as it was probably coming from a bore. I checked it out; it was bore water with a metallic taste about it and I thought that if it was all right for the animals it should be all right for me, so I filled the water bottles and had a good drink. I wonder what chemical preserves my stomach?

On arrival in Morgan I rehydrated with a copious amount of orange juice, and booked in at the hotel, a solid stone two-storey affair, built when Morgan was at the end of a railway line. Produce brought by river boats was loaded onto trains bound for Adelaide. At dinner that night I learnt more about wine. Like many drinkers at the time I believed that white wine was a beverage to be drunk immediately unlike red wine which in many cases improved with age. During the meal I asked the proprietor who was also the waiter for a bottle of wine. He said he had just taken over the hotel and wasn't sure what was available. He invited me to go with him and inspect the underground cellar. It was a stone cellar, beautifully cool and what I would have died for to have at home. The cellar was bare except in one corner there was one case of wine. It contained a dozen bottles of 1968 Orlando Riesling white wine. The hotelier said those would be no good as they were eleven years old. I suggested we try one, so we did, and then a second. The Riesling variety ages beautifully under the right conditions. You learn something new every day.

I pedalled south to the Barossa Valley, visiting some of the wineries I purchased wine from. I had organised a wine club at work which bought wines by the dozen straight from wineries to distribute to members. At one winery I arrived, parked the bicycle against the wall and went in to have a taste. The young lady in the tasting room carefully looked at this scruffy bloke in sweaty T-shirt and shorts and poured me a minimum tasting sip. I told her my name and that I was a regular customer, but I didn't mention that I had just sent them an order for five cases of wine. She disappeared briefly into the office, obviously doing a quick check, and returned all smiles and said, 'Mr Peel, you will want to taste everything.' The next tasting glass held double the amount of the first one. Thankfully I was booked in at the nearby Angaston Hotel for the night, so I was able to taste everything. From the Barossa, after two days of rest in Adelaide, my next opportunity for a taste came in McLaren Vale, again being warmly received by some of the suppliers to the wine club.

My return trip to Melbourne took me onto the main Adelaide –Melbourne link, the Dukes Highway, as there were no parallel minor roads. The truck drivers seemed to have warned each other of the cyclist on the highway and I would get a wave and a toot as they passed. If a truck was approaching me and there was another coming up behind me, the truck I could see flashed its lights and I knew to move to the side. In another incident, just west of Keith, an old station wagon filled with a woman and children came around the bend travelling at high speed but didn't straighten up, going across to the other side of the road before the driver tried to regain control and swerved across to the other side of the road. I knew there was a car behind me so I headed for the grass, giving the car behind me as much room as possible. Eventually the station wagon driver regained control and sped on, passing the other car safely. My guess was that the driver, heading towards Adelaide, had fallen asleep at the wheel trying to do the drive from Melbourne to Adelaide in one day. I hope the family arrived safely. Once in Victoria I was able to use less busy roads to reach Ballarat where the bicycle and I boarded the train to Melbourne.

The cycling bug had well and truly bitten me so in 1980 I undertook my longest trip on two wheels. I had three weeks up my sleeve so I headed north. As usual, to get clear of city traffic and the busy highways, I took the train, this time to Seymour, 100 kilometres north of Melbourne. It was easy going over the next four days as I made my way into New South Wales and Wagga Wagga along quiet country roads. Where possible I chose to stay in hotels rather than motels overnight, as there was generally someone to talk with at the bar. I was regarded as slightly mad but harmless but people were happy to chat. The next night was spent at Temora, an important rail junction town, with the railways being the main reason for its existence. I booked in at the hotel and the meals were served in the main bar. It was obviously a beer-drinking town because when I asked for a bottle of wine with my meal the barman looked a little perplexed and the request also attracted the attention of the other drinkers. The barman dived into a cupboard, produced a bottle of wine and said he hoped it was all right as this was the only wine they had. It wasn't all right, it was a name unfamiliar to me, but it was drinkable, just. With the locals watching, curious about this nutcase on a bicycle drinking wine, there was only one thing to do: look relaxed and drink it with a smile on your face. The next day I had a slight hangover but it soon cleared after a few kilometres of pedalling.

In central western New South Wales there were more hills and occasionally I had to use the very busy Newell Highway. In preparing for this trip I was warned about the sharp burrs from plants in the area and had equipped the cycle with heavy duty thick touring tyres. It was just as well I had, as at various stops I would check the tyres and remove the burrs that would have punctured a normal tyre. I had a day off in Parkes before heading to Dubbo and Gilgandra and then riding through the beautiful Warrumbungle National Park before staying a night in Coonabarabran. The next break for a day was in Tamworth and getting there I again had to use parts of the Newell Highway. From Tamworth I avoided the highway by taking longer back roads to Armidale. It was the longest distance I had ridden in a day, 180 kms, and it was sunny and hot. I was grateful when I ran into a council road crew, working on one of the roads, who provided me with cold, fresh water from the water cooler. From Armidale it was time to head east to the coast to Nambucca Heads. Halfway there I stayed at a village called Ebor and booked in at the local hotel. It was a Sunday and the custom was for all the local families to gather at the hotel on a Sunday afternoon to have drink or a cup of tea or coffee and have a gossip. There was a playground where the children could gather all under the watchful eyes of their parents. It created a friendly, communal atmosphere.

On the way to Nambucca Heads I had to go down a very steep gravel road from Dorrigo at the top of the Great Dividing Range to sea level. The steep descent on the rough gravel resulted in three spokes on the wheels of the bicycle breaking. At Nambucca Heads I asked the hotel proprietor where I could get my spokes replaced. I was told to go to the garage which catered for the trucking industry. The chap there also looked after all the local kids' bicycles. I found the garage and sure enough the chap could replace my spokes straight away, so amongst the Mack and Kenworth semi-trailers my Repco cycle, upside down, was being made roadworthy again. I travelled south more or less along the Pacific Highway reaching Kempsey where, with leave time expiring, it was a case of catching the train to Sydney and the Southern Aurora overnight express to Melbourne.

The following year, 1981, again in October and November, the challenge was a bike ride to Sydney around the coast. This turned out to be shorter but much more difficult than the ride to Northern New South Wales the previous year. This time I had one of my work colleagues, Graeme Parker, to ride with me. My partner, Rob, was definitely not into cycling. Over a week, using minor roads and closely following the coastline, we arrived at Lakes Entrance in eastern Victoria. From there the hard work began with a steep climb out of the town and being forced to use the Princes Highway to eventually get to Orbost. In Victoria the highway was in good condition with smooth gravel edges. To get away from the highway we travelled east from Orbost on a minor road to Bemm River. This eventually turned into a two-wheel sandy track, described by Graeme as a 'goat track'. We weren't game to continue on the track marked on the map with a dotted line, so from Bemm River we returned to the highway and climbed over Mount Drummer in the Alfred National Park before heading to the border with New South Wales past the little settlement of Genoa. At the border sign we stopped for the photo opportunity showing we had got that far.

In New South Wales the Princes Highway changed in character. It was not well maintained. At the edges the bitumen ended with a drop of some centimetres to the rough side gravel. The road was narrow, and when two trucks passed there was very little room for a cyclist. There were no alternative parallel minor roads. We took a day's break at Eden before moving north towards Sydney. After an overnight stop with friends in the Wollongong suburb of Austinmer, we prepared for the steepest part of the trip, the climb from the coast up the escarpment to Stanwell Park. We did this in very low gear and without stopping until we reached the

Cliff at VIC–NSW border, near Genoa, November 1981

lookout used by hang-gliders to launch their flights. We admired the view, congratulated ourselves and got our breaths back. The hills and valleys of the Royal National Park were a breeze after that. We battled the traffic to our hotel near Central Station in Sydney, spent a day doing nothing very much, and then took the Southern Aurora overnight train back to Melbourne. We took our bicycles to the goods van and watched as they were thrown on top of several hundred mail bags bound for Melbourne. We felt the bikes were safe up on top of that load.

On a January weekend the next year, another cycling friend and I decided to have a weekend ride to Wangaratta. My companion, Colin Betts, had been with me on several short weekend rides previously. We intended to get the Friday evening train to Seymour, only to be told the rail motor had broken down and a substitute train would soon arrive. Being Friday night, a replacement train was hard to find. Eventually the motor section of the train was towed away leaving the trailer carriage for the passengers. This was hauled by a 'T' class diesel locomotive which was more used to shunting heavily laden goods trucks around. It felt no pain in hauling this one carriage unit. As a result we had a faster than usual trip to Seymour. The conductor came around to find out at which stations the train needed to stop to allow passengers to get off. At the small stations where no one was getting off, the train slowed down and if no-one was standing on the platform it sped on.

Next day we had a casual ride along the Goulburn River to Shepparton on the quiet road on the west bank of the river. Our destination was Wangaratta, but the heat came down. By the time we got to Benalla we gave up the thought of riding and headed for the swimming hole on the Broken River, happily standing up to our necks in the water cooling off. We then got the evening train at Benalla instead of Wangaratta, back to Melbourne.

In 1982 in the cooler month of March I joined another cycling enthusiast. He was also interested in wine and a student at the Roseworthy Agriculture College, and was interested in a cycle tour of South Australian vineyards. He was Bruce Minchinton who would meet me in South Australia. This time I took my old favourite The Overland train to Adelaide and set off from there. I cycled to his home in Gawler, north of Adelaide, stayed overnight and then in the following days rode around the vineyards in the Clare Valley. We started off our tour in Auburn in pouring rain. By the time we had arrived in Clare after several tastings, despite being soaking wet we weren't feeling too much pain. Due to study commitments Bruce left me in Clare to return to Gawler, arranging to meet me in McLaren Vale south of Adelaide.

I took the opportunity to cycle to the Riverland wine-growing area around Renmark and Loxton before heading south to Murray Bridge on the Murray River. Taking back roads I was making my way to Victor Harbor when, coming around a bend on a track through scrub, I ran in to a large obstacle. It was a big red kangaroo, taller than me, standing in the middle of the track. I stopped, it looked at me, I looked at it, waiting to see what was going to happen next. I'm not sure who was most surprised, me with a big red kangaroo in the way, or it, with a human not in a car but on a strange collection of metal. I don't think too many cyclists came that way. Eventually the way was clear as 'big red' leisurely hopped away.

From Victor Harbor I made my way to McLaren Vale meeting Bruce as planned at the McLaren Vale Hotel. We had booked in for a week at the hotel. Our plan was to visit 40 wineries over four days, ten wineries a day, east, north, west and south of the hotel. We intended riding to the furthest winery in the direction for the day and gradually cycling closer to the hotel, working on the theory that if the tasting became a little too intense we could walk our bicycles from the last wineries on the list to the hotel. This sounded good in theory but we did underestimate the hospitality of some of the wine growers who were providers for my wine club. On one day we rode about 10 kilometres to our furthest winery, it was about ten o'clock when we arrived and the heat of the day was already around the mid-30s mark. Our host watched as we pedalled in, and on walking into the tasting room he said to us, 'You need a drink, not a taste,' and proceeded to pour us generous glasses of cold white wine, a very good start to the day. Thankfully the remaining nine wineries were not as generous.

Bruce Minchinton and signposts, McLaren Vale, April 1982

The hotel was a family-run affair and its dining room was closed on a Sunday. However we were invited to have a meal in the dining room if we were prepared to eat what was being cooked for the family. We had no problem with that. Our host had also brought up several boxes of wine from the cellar to sell on Monday as specials. They included some aged wines that were reaching their use-by date. Our host said we could just help ourselves and leave the empty bottle/s on the table and he would add it/them to the account. What an invitation, good food and two cases of wine! I won't reveal how many empties were left with the dirty dishes but remember, we were fairly young and pretty fit and had been cycling all the week. Justice was done to the offer. Because they were good wines there were no after-effects from a slight over-indulgence. We easily managed the ride back to Adelaide in time for me to catch the overnight train back to Melbourne, the bicycle in the goods van and me in a sleeper.

One does actually have to work so that these expeditions can be financed. Talking of finance, one little incident made me wonder about some people who run businesses. One weekend three of us had cycled to Colac in Victoria's Western District and decided to have a meal while waiting for the afternoon train back to Melbourne. We propped our bicycles against the glass window of a café. The owner came out, very agitated that the bicycles had been placed there. Without comment we took our bicycles and walked to a nearby opposition café, leaned our bicycles against its glass front and went inside to enjoy a three-course meal, which was probably not a bad return on a quiet Sunday afternoon. The other chap didn't have bicycles against his window, but I don't quite know about the customers he did or did not have though.

THIRTEEN

From Land to Air

As mentioned, one has to work and so it wasn't until the following year, 1983, that I was able to journey into the unknown. I accepted an invitation to visit Japan. The background to this was that in 1958 while at the Vincent School of Broadcasting one of my friends was Bill Waters. His main claim to fame until then was representing Australia as a wrestler in the 1956 Olympic Games. Not being able to afford a university education he decided to learn Japanese, working on the theory that as trade increased with the old enemy, translators would be an urgent requirement. He was right and eventually could speak the language fluently. In the course of travelling with executives he met a Japanese air hostess who eventually became his wife. To give their three children the advantage of education in both Australia and Japan, they would live at times in each country. At this time, they were living in Fukui on the west coast of the main island. The adventure started even before I left Australia. I took up an offer of a cheap return flight through Philippine Airlines, booked through an agency near the ABC studios in Melbourne. I had paid my money and was due to pick up my tickets on the day the early morning news reported that the agency had gone broke and a number of customers had lost their money. I was one of the lucky ones, because the agent I had dealt with had managed to get my tickets before everything went feet up and the tickets would be honoured by the airline. I took the opportunity offered by the airline of spending a week in Manila in the Philippines. Before leaving I was warned of the traps waiting for tourists and also that I would be dismayed by the poverty. I was reminded of this sitting near an open window in a small cafe when a young hand reached in from the street and tried to take some rice from a bowl on my table. That was a bit of a shock to the system; not so much the attempted theft, but the desperation.

Not far from Manila is Lake Taal, which contains a not-too-dormant volcano, I had a guide who arranged a local boatman to take us out to the volcano and guide us on to the floor of the crater. This was a hot, nerve-racking walk with gushes of steam popping up every now and again. Arriving back onshore we were invited into the boatman's home which from the outside looked very flimsy, but inside was neat, tidy and had all the modern conveniences including a refrigerator with ice-cold beer. My guide used the local bus services to get us back to Manila. At one stage I wasn't sure that an outing to walk in the crater of a sort of dormant volcano had been a bright idea or not. We had to change buses at cross roads in an isolated part of the bush and I felt a little vulnerable as one bus moved off and my guide and I waited for another bus to appear from a different direction. However it did arrive vaguely on time and I was eventually reunited with my belongings in the capital.

Philippine Airlines flew me to Osaka in Japan where I was met by Bill and his wife Moto. My luggage came off the baggage carousel one item at a time. Somewhere on arrival the vinyl bag

The floor of Taal Volcano, near Manila, Philippines, July 1983

had been ripped open and the contents released. Probably more by good luck than good management nothing was missing but a new bag was needed.

I found it an interesting experience living as a guest in Fukui. I took the opportunity to accompany Moto as she visited the local supermarket. I did attract some attention being a tall European man. Later Moto told me there had been some rather nasty comments in Japanese about my presence. I witnessed another example of anti-foreign feeling when Bill took the family and me to visit a Japanese shrine in the hills near their home. Before we left Bill explained to me that some Japanese, especially in country areas around religious places, can't accept the fact that foreigners could speak their beautiful language − only Japanese could do that. At the parking area at the shrine Bill asked the female parking attendant in fluent Japanese where he should park. She refused to answer him and looked at Moto, waiting for her to speak. She sat silent. Bill repeated his request but again she refused to acknowledge him. In good Australian fashion he let fly with a range of expletives in Japanese and then parked the car in what he hoped was the abbot's parking spot. Judging by the look on her face and the blushes, the parking attendant well and truly understood what was said.

On the visit I was also given the chance of getting within a metre or two or a nuclear generator. Not far south of Fukui is one of Japan's nuclear power stations. We were shown over the station by the manager, returning a favour owed to Bill. Naturally safety is the main concern, especially against contamination. Before the tour began, apart from signing a declaration that no matter what happened it wasn't the power station's fault, we had to strip down to our undergarments, be checked for our radiation levels and were given a heavy protective uniform to wear. After inspecting the control room we were taken to the tanks where the reaction takes place. It was interesting but not spectacular. You could see the tanks, hear the hum and notice the protective shields. Only a few minutes was allowed for a visit so there was not much time to 'ooh' and 'aah'. On return we had to strip to our undergarments, have a shower and then be tested for any extra radiation. My certificate, which we were allowed to keep, showed a miniscule amount of extra radiation, being of no concern. I was told you get more radiation from the microwave oven in the kitchen.

After a fascinating fortnight in Japan the next stop was Hong Kong, then still under the thumb of the British. I did my tourist duty and, for a cheap thrill after taking the cable car to the top of Mount Victoria, I took the local double-decker bus back to sea level. I sat on the top deck next to a window on the passenger side and as the bus passed other traffic and went around bends I admired the view of houses that appeared hundreds of metres directly below the bus. Not a trip for faint hearts or those with a fear of heights. On returning to Australia I flew first to Manila where there was a four-hour wait for the connecting flight to Australia. The few passengers travelling on to Australia were provided with a room at the airport hotel. While waiting I heard a very unfamiliar noise. Looking out across the tarmac I saw a squadron of six World War II Spitfires taking off in formation. Afterwards I learnt that they were doing their tricks as part of a war movie but I never found out which one it was. I was also unable to see the insignia the planes were carrying, so I didn't know which country they represented. It certainly broke the monotony of waiting at an airport.

With Rob having languished at home while I rode a bicycle around South Australia and flew to Japan, it was time for him to join in the fun of exploration. We still had the Renault 12 so we dusted that off and as it was July 1984 there was only one way to go, north. What better way to start the journey than with memories of the first trip we did together the day after we met? We drove to Moulamein in southern New South Wales and booked in once again at Tattersalls Hotel. The Renault 12 purred along beautifully, and it was much easier going through places like the Warrumbungle National Park in a car than on a bicycle. We crossed into Queensland at Mungindi and travelled north through Central Queensland including some of my old stamping grounds when I was working in Rockhampton. Nothing much had changed except I was happy to see more bitumen and less gravel and bulldust on the roads. We purposely stayed inland as we made our way north, eventually to Cooktown. We did take time to admire the natural beauty of North Queensland especially around the Atherton Tableland, and the home-made pies were still being sold at Mount Molloy. The road to Cooktown had improved since the time I took the smaller Renault 10 there some thirteen years previously. Many of the creek crossings had culverts, the bulldust patches had gone but the road was still graded gravel.

Tattersalls Hotel, Moulamein, June 1984

Near Cooktown we diverted to visit the Lions Den Hotel at Helenvale. After about 30 kilometres of rough gravel we arrived at the hotel, a solitary building of corrugated iron that appeared to be held together by wooden posts and good luck. The hotel was originally a watering place for miners but was now a haunt of hardy travellers or a haven for people that have taken a wrong turn, in more ways than one. On the walls and ceiling were business cards of visitors over the years, hundreds of them, including mine.

I imagine many of these cards could tell interesting stories. The beer was cold but not cheap.

The reason we travelled inland to reach Cooktown was because we planned to return to Melbourne along the east coast of Australia. We saw a very different picture of how Australians lived as we passed through the holiday resorts, coastal cities and fishing ports. It is quite a contrast to the vast open spaces and agricultural pursuits away from the sea. We found it a very valuable way to understand our country and its differences. On the way home we stopped for a day in some of the bigger cities to have a look around, including Rockhampton. There we took a drive to Emu Park to visit my old surf club.

The long trip home was enjoyable as we took in the local sights, interesting as we waited for ferries to take us over several large rivers in New South Wales, and included a memorable lunch break at Maclean. We sat down on a lawn on the banks of the Clarence River, which runs through the town, to eat some sandwiches. It was a pleasant grassy slope and I was enjoying my first sandwich. Then I felt a painful bite under my trousers and then another bite moving further north, then another and that's when I realised I had sat on an ants' nest and the occupants weren't happy. There was a public toilet nearby and – to hell with dignity – the pants came down and I fended off the invading ants as best I could. Eventually I won the battle, the ants, or those that survived, retreated, and I put on my ant-free trousers, restored my dignity and finished the sandwiches seated in the car. Rob remained unscathed but highly amused.

Over the next few days we ambled along the coast, surviving Sydney's traffic and winding streets, visited friends in Wollongong and had a taste of the southern New South Wales coastal towns. A much improved Princes Highway took us back to Melbourne. To get the legs back into action I had a couple of weekend cycle trips with my cycling mate, Colin Betts. One was around Ballarat and Maryborough, and the other was into Gippsland where we took the train to Leongatha (the line is now closed), rode onto Phillip Island, took a ferry to Stony Point and a train to get home. By then the legs and the backside were back in riding form.

Early in 1985 we said goodbye to the Renault 12 car and in its place had a brand-new Toyota Corona. I chose this one because it was roomier than the Renault 12, it had good suspension, good road clearance and I could understand the mechanics. This is important when you're in the back of nowhere and something goes wrong. When you can understand how everything works you can generally manage temporary repairs and limp the vehicle back to the nearest garage. In the twenty-first century cars have computerised engines and complicated working systems aimed at 'efficiency' and 'cost saving', but if anything goes wrong a few kilometres off the beaten track, you're in strife.

Naturally you don't leave a brand-new car languishing in the garage, and you have to learn how to drive and tame the beast. Rob and I decided to visit our national capital testing the Toyota's capabilities on the roads through the Snowy Mountains National Park, and testing our map-reading capabilities with Canberra's numerous roundabouts. Several times the driver was told by the navigator to go around the roundabout again as we had missed the turnoff. The new car handled well on the narrow roads leading to the Jenolan Caves and then the sightseeing trips in the Blue Mountains west of Sydney. We returned at a very easy pace, again along the coast having enjoyed our previous journey following the

Princes Highway, but this time staying a little longer at Ulladulla, Bermagui and Merimbula.

I had taken a fishing rod and tackle with me on this trip and at Bermagui I found a good fishing spot near the hotel on the waterfront. I had some good bites and was able to take a basket of fish back to the hotel where the cook was happy to accept them, prepare several for us for our evening meal, put a sign 'fresh local fish' on the dining room blackboard and serve them to other guests. I was glad to see none were wasted. We were very happy with the performance of the new car which was well and truly run in by the time we arrived home.

By October the cycling bug had caught up with me again and I had a couple of weeks' leave up my sleeve so off I rode once again in the direction of Adelaide. I started my ride at Echuca, arriving there by train I headed to Swan Hill again using the river track through the redgum forest beside the Murray, this time well prepared for the mosquitoes. At Murrabit I crossed the Murray into New South Wales and used back roads to reach San Hill. On one lonely stretch I met a mob of sheep. After carefully riding through them I met the drover who asked me if I was in a hurry. When I said that word wasn't in my vocabulary, he suggested that I take a break and keep an eye on the flock as he had to go into nearby Kerang for some urgent equipment. For an hour I became a shepherd. My upbringing on a farm again was helpful although I had no problem with the sheep. There is nothing like riding a bicycle in the countryside for the unexpected to crop up.

From Swan Hill I travelled west with my next overnight stop at Manangatang. The name had always intrigued me so I decided to include it on my itinerary. Sorry, Manangatang, but apart from the name the place was not that much different from other Mallee towns of the same size. The next night I arrived at Underbool in the far west of Victoria. At the hotel I was told the place was booked out. There was a crew from the then PMG's Department working on telephone lines, and there were performers from the Arts Council putting on a local show. The hotelier said there was no other accommodation in town but suggested I go to the local football ground and camp in the umpires' room. It had electricity and a hot shower; the players' rooms had only cold water. The bench was a bit hard to sleep on but there is nothing like a 100-kilometre bike ride to earn a good night's sleep. I had a good dinner and breakfast at the hotel, and the accommodation was free.

I entered South Australia at Pinnaroo and then returned to the Riverland wine country, again staying overnight at Morgan where the hotel this time was well stocked with wine. I arrived in Adelaide from the north and again ran into heavy rain between Auburn and Gawler, where I caught up with my previous cycling partner, Bruce Minchinton. From there I rode to Adelaide and returned to Melbourne as usual on the overnight Overland train. The following year was one of the quietest years I have had for some time as far as travelling was concerned. Some extra responsibilities at work concentrated my mind and limited the scope for disappearing into the distance.

FOURTEEN

Around Australia and the World

The year 1987 was a different matter. By now I had accumulated six months of long-service leave. Unfortunately Rob hadn't been able to do the same with his work so he couldn't share the first part of the long break. By this time I had become quite used to the Toyota and felt quite confident and comfortable in taking it practically anywhere, so what better way of making use of long-service leave but by driving around Australia? I planned a route that would take me to some fairly remote parts of the continent.

With this in mind I equipped the Toyota with heavy duty bar-tread tyres. On the highways they had a unique whine at high speed but they were invaluable on dirt tracks. From previous experience I carried an extra ten litres of petrol and a five-litre container of drinking water. My garage also provided me with spare gaskets, spark plugs and hoses. I was ready to set out alone on this adventure. My first day's drive was a long one from Melbourne to Mildura. After that I limited myself to about 500 miles a day at the most on each stretch. I intended to use a comfortable bed at either a hotel or motel each night, but just in case I carried a one-man tent and a sleeping bag. It was plain sailing west across to Port

Augusta and around the Eyre Peninsula. I made a point of visiting Coffin Bay, and I enjoyed the oysters from its waters.

From Ceduna I crossed the Nullarbor Plain, 80 kilometres of it by road, but the rest of the long stretch across South and Western Australia is through scrub. (If you want to see the real Nullarbor Plain you must travel by train which runs some 400 kilometres to the north and crosses 800 kilometres of the Nullarbor.) There is a roadhouse with fuel, food and accommodation about every 150 kilometres so that was no problem. When the road got close to the cliffs of the Great Australian Bight it was possible to drive to a viewing point close to the cliff face. As there was no fence or barrier of any sort I pondered about the number of cars and bodies that could be in the sea some 200 to 300 metres below. Gruesome thought.

As I crossed into Western Australia the local police had a way of finding out who was arriving on their patch. Travelling at a sedate

Cliffs, Great Australian Bight, Nullabor, June 1987

96 kilometres an hour, the ideal cruising speed for the Toyota, a police car approached me from the opposite direction, did a U-turn behind me and then pulled me over, saying I was speeding. This I politely denied. You are not impolite to police when you are some thousand-odd kilometres from headquarters. I explained I was just a tourist. They examined my licence, told me to watch the speed signs and to move on. The same thing happened a few years later when Rob was driving. As we left Eucla I warned him we would be pulled up for speeding, and we were, in exactly the same manner.

At Norseman I turned north from the highway to Perth and ended up in Kalgoorlie. I met up with a Swedish chap who was touring Australia on a motorcycle. He and I both wanted to see the two-up game in the bush at Kalgoorlie. Briefly, two-up is an Australian invention going back to the mining camps of the nineteenth century, in which two coins, generally two copper pennies, are placed on a board, called a kip, and tossed in the air. You bet against another person whether the coins will land with both heads or tails face up. Under most circumstances it is illegal. This 'illegal' game has been played more or less daily in Kalgoorlie since the beginning of the twentieth century, if not earlier. The one strict rule at this game is that it does not operate on the miners' payday. A cardboard sign on the main road north points you to the dirt track leading into it, which winds its way between the trees. It's interesting to watch the tourist buses lurch their way in. On the site alcohol is banned both for sale and drinking. There is no electricity and the ring has no roof. Protection from the wind was by a brush and tin wall around the arena. On the rare occasions it rains in Kalgoorlie, play is suspended. Games end at sunset. I think one of us made a profit of $10. It was a bit of fun. I can understand why it is banned. It is very hard for the promoters to make a profit, and it would be very difficult if not impossible to tax, therefore it must be immoral.

From Kalgoorlie the road took me north through the mining areas of Leonora and Wiluna to Meekatharra, staying overnight in the grand two-storey hotel built many years ago in some mining boom time. From Meekatharra I turned west to head to the coastal town of Carnarvon. The 'road' is actually an occasionally graded gravel track with no culverts over the dry creek crossings. The heavy duty tyres on the Toyota proved their worth. Halfway to Carnarvon I stayed overnight at Gascoyne Junction. It's a small settlement with a hotel which had a spare room for me.

That night, a couple of country and western singers were putting on a show in the main bar, probably the biggest space in the village. There were only a few people there when I arrived and I wondered where the audience would come from. After dinner they appeared from out of the bush in a variety of four-wheel drives and soon there were a good sixty people crowded into the bar. Helping the barman serve the drinks was the local policeman in full uniform. Later, when I asked him about it, he said that many policemen in one-man stations acted as barmen on these occasions. He said that when he was behind the bar in uniform there was never any trouble in front of the bar. That made sense. The singers, a man with a guitar and a woman with a violin, put on a very entertaining performance.

The next morning at breakfast they told me their story. For many years the man and his wife had travelled the highways and byways of the west performing at pubs and clubs. About a year ago his wife had become ill and couldn't continue so his wife's sister offered to fill in for a month while she took a break from her secretarial job. At the end of the month the wife was unable to resume performing. The stand-in had enjoyed the month's travel so much she told me it was a great break from office work and she was happy to continue touring. In her words she said she told her old boss in more or less polite terms what he could do with the job, and hadn't looked back since. It was one of those nights you don't expect and it adds to the enjoyment of travelling.

I reached the coast, and crossed the Gascoyne River which in the dry season is a gentle stream meandering through vast beds of sand and in the wet season a roaring torrent of water covering the wide flood plain. I headed north on the North West Coastal Highway, turning off the highway to visit Exmouth and see at close hand the huge North West Cape radio masts. Further north I took another detour to the port of Onslow, diverting slightly to visit the ruins of the original port of Onslow and found there was very little to see. Booked in for the night at the local hotel, right on dusk I noticed from the first floor a truck going along the main street sending out a huge spray of what looked like water but was actually liquid mosquito repellent. The proprietor told me this happened regularly as Onslow was built on very swampy ground and this was how the council controlled the mosquito population. It seemed to have worked; I did not hear a mosquito during the night.

The extent of mining in Western Australia was evident the further north I went heading towards Port Hedland. On the way there is a roadhouse at Whim Creek, one of the few watering holes between Dampier and Port Hedland. Beside the service centre there was a very large and strong container firmly held down by iron beams and cables. It was the roadhouse's cyclone shelter where the local inhabitants go when a cyclone blows through.

Dry season creek crossing, Carnarvon–Meekathara
Road, Gascoyne Junction, June 1987

Hotel, Gascoyne Junction, June 1987

As I was waiting to use the petrol pump the man in front of me accidentally filled his car up with diesel instead of petrol. He had driven in with a wife and three children who appeared to be very tired. They had had a long day of travelling and, as he explained to me, he wasn't concentrating. He asked me what he should do and first I told him not to start the engine and asked if the petrol tank could be drained. He said it could, so we pushed the car to a spot where the garage proprietor said it was all right to drain the diesel. We then pushed the car back to the bowser and this time he made sure he got the right hose into the tank. We assumed the petrol would have absorbed any residue of diesel and sure enough it worked. His car was mobile again. The only trouble was he had to pay for a tank full of diesel as well as a tank full of petrol.

A day later, on my way from Port Hedland to Broome, I ran into another traveller with petrol problems. This time it was at Sandfire Flat, another of the watering places. A motorcyclist was filling up his petrol tank and he asked me if I knew where the next petrol station was. I told him that it was in Broome, nearly 400 kilometres further on. This concerned him as he wasn't sure if his tankful would be enough for him to get here. I suggested he stick to the most economical speed for the motorcycle and, since he was leaving ahead of me, to watch for my car if he ran out of fuel as I carried extra petrol, and I would be able to provide him with enough to get to Broome. He did make it to Broome because I ran into him at the famous Roebuck Hotel. He said he did not have much fuel left in the tank when he arrived.

After some rest and recreation in Broome which included a swim at Cable Beach, I moved onto Derby and used part of the Gibb River Road to reach the Windjana Gorge. After saying hello to the freshwater crocodiles sunbaking on the banks of the gorge,

I gave the Toyota a good test, using a station track to cut across to Tunnel Creek National Park. This was a two-wheel dirt track and each time there was a dry watercourse the track went down the bank, crossed the dry bed and went up the other bank. At two of them I was a bit concerned because the banks were fairly steep. In both cases I parked the car on the bank, walked down testing the firmness of the track, particularly when going up the other side, hoping my tyres could get enough traction to keep the car moving. I decided it was all right. I gently eased the car down the slope and across the bed and then started the climb out. The bar-treads did their job and, using bottom gear, I reached the top. Going up the bank all I could see was the sky through the windscreen. I felt some relief as the front wheels went over the edge of the bank and the country came into view. My confidence in the Toyota to handle difficult terrain grew after those experiences.

After doing the tourist bit wading through Tunnel Creek I was preparing to leave when a man in a four-wheel drive station wagon, who had just driven in from Fitzroy Crossing, asked me if he could get through to Windjana Gorge. I pointed to my rear-wheel drive Toyota and said I managed to get this through and with a four-wheel drive he shouldn't have too much of a problem. He seemed happy and I hope he made it all right.

I stayed the night in a donga at the Fitzroy Crossing Hotel. Dongas are portable sleeping quarters used in mining camps, hotels and similar establishments. This particular donga was a large shipping container converted into a comfortable bedroom with a wash basin. They are quite common in the outback of Australia. There were several people staying at the hotel and it was suggested to us that, if we wanted a few drinks after the evening meal, to have them in the back bar as the local indigenous people took over the front bar and tended to be noisy and occasionally a bit excitable. Being curious I had a look at the front bar before the evening rush. The whole room was painted a dark grey with a concrete floor, and the heavy metal tables and bar stools were welded into the floor. The bar, and the staff behind it, were protected by a heavy steel mesh open enough for money and drinks to be exchanged. From the more sedate back bar I can vouch that the local inhabitants noisily enjoyed the refinements of the front bar. The performance was repeated the following night as I spent the day visiting nearby Geikie Gorge.

Before starting this epic tour I was more than once warned about travelling in the outback and being prepared for emergencies, hence the extra water, petrol and spare tyres. On my way from Fitzroy crossing to Halls Creek I was hailed by a car which had broken down and I was asked if I could help. The car was certainly not new and looked in not particularly good condition. What concerned me was that the three people in the car where not carrying any water, just relying on a bottle or two of soft drink. I offered to take one of them into Halls Creek to get help, but a motorist travelling the other way, who had also stopped, offered to take the man into Fitzroy Crossing which was closer. That group certainly was not prepared for the hazards of outback travel.

While driving on the Great Northern Highway as it is known in the Kimberley, occasionally I came across a straight section of the highway with a white line drawn across it and then about 100 metres further on a similar white line. In between there were no guideposts and the bitumen had been widened. On inquiring I learnt that these sections were used as emergency landing strips for the Royal Flying Doctor planes attending serious road accidents.

A space was also cleared beside the road so that the plane could be moved off the highway while the doctor treated patients, and the road could be re-opened to let traffic through before being closed for the plane to take off again. From Halls Creek I travelled north to Wyndham, admired the Ord River scheme to the east and wondered how the huge storage of water in Lake Argyle could be fully utilised. Thirty years later I am still wondering.

I left Western Australia and drove into the Northern Territory taking in Darwin and Kakadu National Park. I was aware of the long distances involved but that was not so for some of the overseas tourists I met in Darwin who were under the impression that Kakadu was just a short drive away and the whole tour of the park could be done in a day. I spent three days in Kakadu on my visit and only saw a small section of this magnificent park.

From Darwin the next national park I visited was Katherine Gorge. To get some good aerial photos I hired a helicopter for a short flight. At the appointed time I made my way to the helipad and muttered to myself, 'I bet I end up with a New Zealand cropdusting pilot.' At the helipad my first guess was right; the accent gave him away as a Kiwi. I started chatting to him and yes, he had just come across and he volunteered that his main job in New Zealand was cropdusting. Two out of two for intuition. I had told the booking office that I wanted to take some photos. They were very good and had taken off the passenger door of the aircraft so I would have a great view. This was a bit disconcerting until we took off and I found that despite whatever angle the horizon was, the centre of gravity was inside the helicopter and there was no feeling of sliding out – a lesson in physics I was not taught at school. He was a very good pilot and I got some great photographs.

Cliff in a Bell helicopter, Katherine Gorge, July 1987

An overnight stop at Mataranka, a swim in the hot springs, and a chance meeting with cycling pal, Colin Betts, on his way north, broke the journey to Camooweal. Just before leaving the Northern Territory, I kept a look out for the roadhouse at Frewena where years before I had met the newlyweds from Tennant Creek. There was no sign of the old roadhouse, just the rather barren landscape, and only memories remained. The Barkly Highway hadn't changed much; it was still a narrow strip of bitumen with gravel edges and still living up to its reputation as a 'crystal highway'. After Mount Isa I turned south to head for Birdsville on what was described as the Channel Country Development Road. This was a broad gravel road covered in gibber, which means large stones and pebbles, giving the Toyota suspension a real workout. (At the end of the trip the shock absorbers had to be replaced.) There was also a continuous clang as the tyres threw the stones up against the mudguards. I stopped overnight at Boulia and didn't see the mythical Min Min lights despite the signs in the town assuring me that I would.

My vision of Birdsville before I arrived was of an outback village away from any sign of civilisation. This vision disappeared when I approached the town and saw the tall microwave link tower. In the centre of town was a Telecom telephone booth with links to the rest of the world. Birdsville had caught up with the world and the television reception at the hotel was better quality than I was getting at the time in East Hawthorn. I couldn't stay at the hotel as it was full of tourists so I had to camp in the caravan park. This was easier said than done as most of the park was on top of solid rock. I was eventually able to drive some tent pegs into cracks within the rock and pitched my small tent which sagged woefully in the middle. One compensation was that the showers at the ground were supplied by plentiful bore water at just the right temperature. Because of the minerals in the water it was a very relaxing shower. Despite the sleeping bag being on a bed of stone I slept well. On the way out from Birdsville I saw the road sign indicating the Birdsville Track to Maree and made a mental note to take the Toyota along it sometime in the future. I was sure the Toyota would cope with reasonable conditions on the track.

Heading homewards over the next few days I wandered through south-west Queensland including some areas I knew from my days working in Charleville. I crossed from Queensland to New South Wales from Cunnamulla, spending the night in Bourke. From Bourke I called into Lightning Ridge keeping in mind the opal mining I had seen at Cooper Pedy. Like Cooper Pedy, the land around Lightning Ridge was pockmarked with mine shafts as miners tried their luck but the houses there were

Camping ground, Birdsville, July 1987

above ground. At Pokolbin I caught up with another cycling mate, Bruce Minchinton, who was now working at a local winery. It was good to catch up on travelling news and of course sample the local wines.

After leaving Pokolbin I experienced the first problem with the car, a slow tyre leak, which allowed me to drive to a garage at Cessnock and have the tyre quickly repaired without getting my hands dirty. There was only one other incident and that happened on the Hume Highway near Wangaratta when, on a section under repair, a passing truck threw up a stone which took a small chip out of my windscreen. Arriving home with a car showing all the travelling stains of a long journey over a variety of roads covering 17 000 kilometres, and only two minor repairs, I felt the Toyota Corona had earnt its keep. The best way to learn about your country is to travel around it.

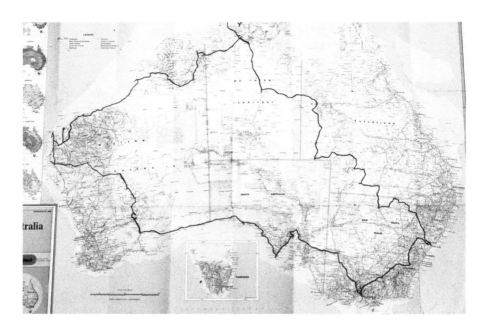

Map of around Australia trip, 1987

I still had half of my long-service leave left and Rob had arranged to take his annual leave so it could coincide with my break. My sister was living in Reading in England and two of my work colleagues, who Rob knew well, wanted us to visit them in Greece. In a bit of high-powered decision making, we worked out that I would take trains as best I could to get to Reading overland, and Rob, when his holidays began, would fly over and meet me there. We would have a look around and then stay with our friends in Athens from where we would fly home using Olympic Airways. Planning this epic rail trip meant using a travel agent to arrange hotel bookings and also dealing with the bureaucratic problems of travelling through Communist China, Mongolia and the then Soviet Union. My travel arrangements in China, Mongolia and the Soviet Union were handled by the Chinese government tourist agency and Intourist in the Soviet Union, giving me no choice of hotels.

To begin my rail journey I flew to Hong Kong and then caught the train to Guangzhou. Crossing the border into China was easier than I expected but I did not anticipate the confusion or the crowds at the Guangzhou station as I boarded the overnight Beijing Express. As a result I missed the call to change my money into local currency which I needed on the train. Luckily a couple of English-speaking students in the compartment happily gave me some local money for some American dollars. On the train I had a bunk and was able to buy some food but was unable to cope with the squat toilet at the end of the carriage. I was relieved, in more ways than one, when I booked into my hotel in Beijing.

The next stage was crossing Mongolia which took 24 hours by train, arriving at the Chinese–Mongolian border at midnight and crossing the Mongolian–Soviet border 24 hours later, again in the middle of the night. To enter Mongolia the only place I could get a visa was at the Mongolian embassy in Beijing. For the 24 hours I was to be in the country, the Mongolian government wanted five passport photographs so I presume that even now somewhere in the Mongolian government archives there are five photographs of me. Before leaving Australia my travel agent said I could spend four hours having a look around the Mongolian capital Ulan Bator while the train was in the station on a tour organised by the government tourist organisation. This would cost US$450. Expensive as it was, I decided I would do the tour as it would probably be the only time I would visit Ulan Bator. A few days later my agent said the government had increased the price to US$950 so that plan was dropped.

I duly went to the Mongolian embassy in Beijing to get my visa, along with the five photographs and US$10 to pay for the visa. I could come back in two days and collect the visa or if I was in a hurry I could pay another US$10 and collect it the next day. As I was spending four days in Beijing I saved the money. I soon found out that the unofficial currency in China and the Soviet Union was American dollars. The last thing local merchants wanted was foreigners to pay for goods in the local currency when they had valuable American dollars. In due course I boarded the Trans–Mongolian Express which would take me through Mongolia to Irkutsk in Siberia. A standard gauge line took the train to the border station of Erenhot. There the carriages were lifted and the standard gauge bogies, which house the train wheels, replaced with the broad gauge bogies, so the train could travel on the Soviet rail network. Some years earlier the broad gauge line extended to Beijing but when relations between China and the Soviets deteriorated, the Chinese replaced the line to the border with a standard gauge track. Passengers had the choice of staying in the carriage as the bogies were being replaced, going to an observation platform to watch the operation, or go to a station café for a cup of tea or coffee. I chose the cafe.

The first taste of bureaucratic madness that had taken over communist Mongolia and the Soviet Union became evident soon after entering Mongolia. Before leaving Beijing travellers at the hotel had warned us of taking any reading matter into Mongolia as the authorities were paranoid about propaganda. To counter this we should have some harmless papers in the compartment so they wouldn't start searching our luggage. The four people in our compartment, two middle-aged Australian ladies and a man from Canada, took notice of this and scattered around a few tourist brochures issued by the Chinese government. Sure enough two border police arrived, inspected our passports and visas and then asked if we were carrying any literature. We said the only thing we had were the brochures on the table. They inspected them seriously and then went away. Soon after two young ladies wearing uniforms with a red cross on their blouses wanted to see our health certificates. This was the first we had heard of this requirement. I suspected that this was just a way to give them a job – 'there is no unemployment in a good communist country'. I said to my companions, 'Just show them any document that looks official and is in English.' This we did. They inspected my piece of yellow paper with black print on it, held it upside down and handed it back to me. The documents from my other companions were also seriously perused and then they smiled and departed. All this was happening between midnight and two o'clock in the morning, so there was not too much sleep that night.

In the morning we woke to a view of grass-covered plains dotted with small villages, a direct contrast to heavily populated China. We stopped for four hours as scheduled in Ulan Bator and from what other passengers told me after they had paid their $950 and done the tour, it really hadn't been worth the cost. For the remainder of the day the train rolled on across the Mongolian steppes and again we crossed the border at midnight to enter the Soviet Union. The border check was very short and easy. The authorities knew exactly who was aboard the train.

That morning I really got the sense of being a world traveller when I sat in the dining car for breakfast and looked across Lake Baikal as the train skirted the southern shore of this inland sea. At Irkutsk, with a day to spare, Intourist offered a day's trip on the lake and a visit to a small Siberian village. The cost was US$25.

I accepted, paid the lady US$26 and waited for my change. She rummaged around a big tin filled with foreign coins and after a few minutes proudly produced 50c and 20c Australian coins, equal at the time to one American dollar.

I left Irkutsk the following day on board the Trans–Siberian Express on an amazing railway line that stretches from the far eastern shore of Siberia across Russia to Moscow, some 6000 kilometres of double track and electrified line. I was told that there were Trans–Siberian Expresses running four times a day in each direction. Apart from expensive local flights the train was the only way to travel as there were no major highways. This was particularly the case in winter when even airports are put out of action. After leaving towns on the journey there is very little to see from the train as on each side of the railway there are long plantations of trees. Apparently these are essential in winter to block snowdrifts from closing the line. There were again four people in my compartment, the two Australian ladies I had met on the Trans–Mongolian Express and a Russian engineering student who could speak quite good English. I had an English–Russian phrase book which gave me a chance to communicate in very basic Russian when it was necessary. The washbasin and toilets were at each end of the carriage and thankfully the toilets were the sit-on ones, not the squat ones I found on the Beijing Express in China. We negotiated with the two ladies the times when privacy was needed before bedding down for the night. In the next compartment were two Russian female students and two young Australian men. The men ran a grocery store in Southern New South Wales.

As there are up to ten time zones across Russia and Siberia, all trains ran on Moscow time so there was no confusion. The confusion came when working out when to go for breakfast and an evening meal. The dining car opened at nine o'clock local time, closed for the staff lunch between noon and one o'clock and closed again at five o'clock. The problem was finding out what the local time was in the morning and not leaving it too late for dinner. So our lot, or those that wanted to, would go for breakfast at ten and dinner at four working out that if we got the time wrong there was a chance the dining car was open. Not that there was much to choose from! At the table you were presented with a huge menu which had about four items with the price marked in pencil. In the end you had black bean soup and borsch with fruit juices. No alcohol was served on the train. The fruit juices, mainly from stone fruit, were quite good.

I brought on board a bottle of vodka for a nightcap. In conversation with a Chinese tourist, I swapped a nip of vodka for a nip of Chinese brandy. I did not get the better of the deal. By the third day on board we had got to know some of our fellow travellers including the Australian chaps and the two Russian students who suggested we have something decent to eat by having a picnic, a word the ladies took from the English–Russian language guide. At the large stations the train stopped for about 15 minutes. On the platform a number of stalls run by locals sold pickled vegetables and cold cooked meat. Under the guidance of our local travellers we purchased a selection of these goodies and brought them aboard. The conductor warned us that after 15 minutes the train would move off without warning so we had to watch the clock carefully. Meanwhile the two grocery chaps had brought some of their products with them, having travelled through the Soviet Union before, and knew the value of some food items. They presented the conductor with a large tin of Australian ham and as a result we had all the crockery and cutlery we needed from the dining car for the picnic. The food and the comradeship went down well despite the Cold War between politicians in 1987.

The Cold War may have played out in the seats of power but certainly not between the Russian people and their overseas visitors. For example, after arriving in Moscow I was wandering around one of the suburban areas and ran into our conductor walking with his wife and two children. I was greeted warmly and introduced to his family. It was a very pleasant experience.

Intourist had booked me into the Como Hotel, a severe 1930s-style establishment. It was bleak but comfortable except that the hot water supply was unreliable. A rule I quickly put into action was that as soon as I went into my room, I turned on the hot water tap. If there was hot water I stripped off and had a shower while the going was good.

Dining was another interesting experience. When I entered the prescribed restaurant for tourists there was always a bunch of waiters standing around in the corner doing nothing. You went to the receptionist who eventually directed you to a table, giving you the feeling that this was a privilege for which you should be immensely grateful, although there would be only three or four other people actually dining in a room with a vast expanse of tables. Like the train, there was a large menu with little choice. If a price was written in pencil beside the item, it may be available. After the third try, I was told the chicken Kiev was available so that is what I had. It was nourishment if nothing else. It was served by one of the two waiters who were actually looking after the diners. As a local explained to me on the quiet, in the Soviet Union everyone had a job. Whether they contributed anything was different matter.

Ensconced in Hotel Como, with an occasional hot shower, I took the advice of an Intourist brochure to enjoy the view from a tall transmission tower. It sounded interesting and I hoped to get some great photographs of Moscow. I found my way to the tower and was about to pay the 10 roubles to go to the top, but was told I couldn't take my camera for security reasons. Why advertise the view if you can't take a photo of it? I put it down to bureaucracy gone mad. Incidentally on my travel documents I was permitted to wander around Moscow unaccompanied but had to notify Intourist if I wanted to travel more than 28 kilometres from the city centre.

My next leg of the rail journey from Moscow to Leningrad (thankfully now restored to its original name, Saint Petersburg) required four more pieces of paper. I was also issued with another four pieces of paper to travel from Leningrad to Helsinki in Finland. I arrived in Leningrad on the overnight train and booked into my allocated hotel. There I had to go to the Intourist desk and confirm my rail journey to Helsinki in three days' time. I handed the clerk the pieces of paper that I thought represented the ticket to Helsinki. The girl looked at the papers and said I had to pay another fare because the papers weren't right. The supervisor was called, a large well-fed local lady who could speak good English. I explained that I had already paid the fare through Intourist. She explained I had only three of the four pieces of paper required. She asked me which hotel I had stayed in while in Moscow and which train I took to get to Leningrad. She then told me to see her in two days' time and she would have the problem solved. After two days of sightseeing, and falling in love with the city, I returned to the Intourist desk. There I was proudly presented with my rail ticket to Helsinki by the smiling supervisor. The errant piece of paper had been torn off accidentally as the conductor on the Moscow–Leningrad train took my ticket. These tickets had been sent back to Moscow, where my missing piece of paper was located and returned to Leningrad by train. A hotel driver picked it up from the station and all four pieces were reunited, allowing me to take the train to Helsinki. A victory for bureaucracy, not common sense.

I duly boarded the train of only three carriages pulled by a diesel engine, along with about 30 other passengers, including a Finnish woman from Helsinki whose husband worked in Leningrad. At the border town of Vyborg the train stopped just short of the station. From the carriage window I could see a 4- to 5-metre tall wire fence stretching into the distance with about 100 metres of cleared land beyond it, reaching to the Finnish forest. As we waited, armed soldiers searched underneath the train, tramped across its roof and came into our compartment, unscrewed the ceiling panels and peered in. I had to leave the compartment and stand in the corridor as the officer interviewed my travelling companion. She then stood outside while my papers and passport were checked and my two bags of luggage, my pockets and my wallet were thoroughly searched. On my companion's return, she said this always happened and because her husband was Russian and she was Finnish they always gave her a rigorous check. It was the most severe border crossing check I have ever experienced. The train then moved a few metres to the station where we had to surrender all Russian currency in exchange for Finnish Marka. I was allowed to keep a five-kopek coin worth less than one cent. The train, still driven by the Russian crew, then crept very slowly over the cleared no-man's land, but as soon as the engine reached the Finnish forest the driver accelerated as hard as the engine could stand. I have often wondered if this was a statement from the driver about the conditions in the 'communist paradise'.

On our arrival at the Finnish border town of Luumaki the contrast was extreme. At the checkpoint three unarmed uniformed officials bordered the train asked for passports, examined them and in my case said in English, 'Welcome to Finland.' All over in a few minutes. The Russian engine was replaced by a Finnish electric engine as most of the network was electrified.

On this leg of my trip, through the Scandinavian countries of Finland, Sweden and Norway, everything appeared to run to clockwork; the hotels had hot water and cameras could be taken anywhere. I also had a Scandinavian rail pass, a very handy purchase I had made before leaving Australia. In Helsinki I was determined to try some reindeer meat until I saw the price on a window menu. I settled for a meal in a Greek café off the beaten track where the proprietor was intrigued to have an Australian as a customer. His story was that his father ran a restaurant in Greece and three of his sons also wanted to run restaurants, so he helped one son start a restaurant in Sydney and the other, my host, a restaurant in Helsinki after helping his brother in Australia.

At Kemi on the border between Sweden and Finland the rail gauge changes to standard so that meant a new train after my overnight stay. I also learnt that prices in these countries were very high for most items taking into account the exchange rate for Australian currency. Eating and drinking needed a cautious approach to keep within my travel budget. I was very pleased I had pre-paid all my accommodation and as many of the other expenses as practicable. I crossed the Arctic circle on my way to the northern town of Narvik in Norway. The train slowed down as it crossed the Arctic circle into the frigid zone so tourists could take photographs of the circle marker. I was prepared for cold weather in Narvik but the temperature was a balmy 15°C. I wasted my time and energy carrying a heavy overcoat that I had expected to use that far north.

The railway to Narvik came from Sweden but to travel south I had to use the bus to get to the next rail terminus at Bode. On the bus that follows the coastline, four young women were sitting behind me. They started talking to each other in English with a very familiar accent. They were Australian girls having a tour they had organised visiting some of the islands off the Norwegian coast. On my travels I have never been surprised about where Australians turn up. I returned to Sweden and from the capital Stockholm I travelled to Goteborg where I was met by the Swedish motorcycle rider I had befriended in Kalgoorlie. He and his friends repaid me with some Swedish hospitality at a newly opened bar in a nearby village. From there I had to get a local night train back to my hotel in Goteborg. The hospitality was good, too good. I missed the last train by a few minutes. As a result I spent the night on a station platform seat until the first train at five o'clock the next morning. I would have preferred the hotel bed. The next day I left Sweden for the Norwegian capital Oslo. After two days I headed west for the North Sea port of Bergen. Between the two cities is a village on the shore of one of the fjords called Flam. My mother had visited this spot and insisted I should also visit Flam. Before I left Australia I booked a night at the hotel. It was quite an expensive overnight stay. On the way to Bergen the train stops at Myrdal, right on top of a range from where a branch line descends to Flam. This is a remarkable piece of engineering. The line, 24 kilometres long, descends to the fjord through one spiral tunnel and some steep grades and also passes close to a waterfall. A group of us had four hours to wait for the train to make its journey. The two-carriage train was at the station and we were invited to sit in it out of the cold. The conductor then came along and said we were getting a bonus as the train would be used to take some workmen to a village halfway down the mountain and we were welcome to stay aboard. We then returned to Myrdal to wait for the train to arrive from Bergen before our train travelled down to Flam. Late in the afternoon the Flam train began its journey down the mountainside to the station on the shore of the fjord.

Freitheim Hotel, Flam, Norway, October 1987

By this time it was dark and fortunately my hotel was close to the railway station. It was the beginning of October and there was only one small light above the door of the hotel. It looked very closed, but I knocked on the door and it was opened by a man who asked, in English, if I was the Mr Peel from Australia. I said yes, I was and he ushered me in. He told me that the hotel had closed at the end of September, the end of the tourist season, but they had one booking from Australia and the caretaker, to whom I was talking, agreed to look after this lone visitor. I now realised why the booking had cost so much, $240 for dinner, bed and breakfast. A lot of money in 1987. He showed me to my room, the best in the house, which had big windows overlooking the fjord. I joined him for a hearty dinner laid out smorgasbord style, had a stroll around the village and then went to bed.

As the sun rose I woke up and watched a light show that made every cent I had paid for the stay more than worthwhile. For about an hour I watched as the sun first lit up the snow on the peaks of the nearby mountains. Then the sunlight moved down into the valley lighting up the forest and then the water in the fjord with colours changing all the time. To me it was one of those once-in-a-lifetime experiences, sheer magic! After another hearty repast I thanked my host and caught the morning train to Myrdal where I waited for the train to Bergen. For the first time on this trip I made use of the heavy overcoat I had lugged from Australia as the first of the winter snows sprinkled the platform.

From Bergen I took the overnight ferry to Newcastle on Tyne in England. Luckily I had a cabin to myself. The first sign of trouble was the duty-free drinks on the ferry. In Scandinavia liquor is heavily taxed so very soon I was with a party of Norwegians who, like me, were taking the opportunity of drinks at a price one could afford. The second sign was one of those North Sea storms that can spring to life without too much warning. The ferry tossed and turned as did my stomach and that was why I was glad I had the cabin to myself. The next morning I was not in peak condition as I went through English customs dealing with an officer who thought this 51-year-old was sneaking into England to work.

View of the Aurlandsfjorden from the village of Flam, Norway, October 1987

When I told him I already had a job and was on long-service leave I don't think he knew what that sort of leave it was. Anyhow, I was grudgingly allowed in, found the hotel I was booked in at and slept well that night. The next morning, buying my train ticket, I learnt what price the English were paying because their railways had been sold off to the highest bidder. I felt I had bought the train, not just a seat on it to get me to Reading.

My sister, Lynnette, found me at Reading station and the following day we found Rob at Heathrow after he flew in from Australia via Greece. After a couple of days of rest and sightseeing, Rob and I commandeered Lynnette's car and had a look around south-west England. More than once we did several circuits at roundabouts on the motorway trying to find the right turn-off. We found the local roads were literally crammed in between stone or wire fences and to stop and photograph a thatched-roofed cottage meant blocking all traffic. Thankfully most traffic appeared to favour the motorways. We also discovered how short distances were between villages and other places worth seeing, unlike Australia where 100 kilometres is only a short distances between photo stops.

To give Rob a brief chance to see Paris we took up an offer of a cheap four-day trip. This was budget travel at its best. Arriving at Gatwick airport we were bussed out to a little Vickers Viscount parked on the far side of the airfield, obviously well out of sight of other international tourists. We boarded it and found we were seated against the pilots' cabin with our backs to the engine facing the rest of the passengers, so we flew backwards into France. As arranged we were transported by bus from the airport, a small one some 50 kilometres from Paris, to our hotel in the city centre. It was early evening as we headed off. On the way, the main highway was blocked by police who directed the bus onto one of the local roads. This was unfamiliar territory for the driver so his assistant stood beside him with a road map working out where we were and how we could get to Paris. After a tour of some villages, unfortunately for us passengers all more or less in the dark, we were delivered to our hotel.

We were shown to our room, which was filled by a large double bed with just enough room to walk around it and a small bathroom with a toilet and washbasin. It was clean, it was cheap, it was in the centre of Paris and the croissants for breakfast were delicious. We didn't complain. On returning from a trip to Versailles, we decided to take a local bus back to Paris and as we went around the Arc de Triomphe in peak hour we marvelled at the skill of the Parisian drivers as, with millimetres to spare, they navigated their cars through the five lanes of the roundabout around the monument, and marvelled even more at the occasional cyclist that joined the throng.

After a week of enjoying my sister's hospitality and seeing other parts of the country, we flew to Greece to catch up with our friends living in Athens, Tony and Elaine Wilson, two journalists whom I worked with in the ABC newsroom. The first night we were in Athens was the eve of the Melbourne Cup and we were invited to attend the Greece–Australia Association's Calcutta night. The Calcutta is a betting system based on the horses running in a particular race. The Australian beer and the Four 'n' Twenty meat pies flown in for the occasion made me feel quite nostalgic.

One of the aspects we noticed was that Athens drivers appeared to be quite suicidal. On a trolley bus we held on grimly as the driver shouted obscenities at the driver of a car beside him as we travelled at a furious rate along one of the streets. The argument was all Greek to me, pardon the pun. On a day cruise visiting some of the Greek islands we shared the ship with a large number of tourists from Japan. What intrigued Rob and me was that every time a person took a photograph, his or her partner wanted to be in it. One incident that made me laugh was watching a man taking a photograph of the village from the wharf. His female companion, on the other side of the wharf, turned around, saw him aiming the camera, and raced across to be in the shot.

We had a very good sample of Greek hospitality when Tony and Elaine suggested we go to one of their favourite restaurants. On arrival we found it had been booked out by a wedding party. As there was a spare table the host of the wedding party invited us to stay and use the table. Most Greeks seem to have some relatives in Australia and it wasn't long before guests were asking us about the country. We then slowly got integrated into the party and were generously and amply provided with retsina, a popular Greek wine. In the early hours Rob showed enough confidence to join in the dancing, Greek style.

Tony and Elaine had a young female cat. The following night there was a terrible yowling from outside their apartment. A randy tomcat had spotted the female and was making its desires known. Rob went into attack mode and, with an empty bottle in hand, went to the defence of the Wilsons' cat. Both disappeared into the night with Rob returning shortly with the bottle still in hand, and the tom nowhere in sight or sound, presumably seeking easier conquests. Finally after a fun-filled and hectic stay we had to head back to Australia on the Olympic Airways flight.

We intended to get to the airport about an hour before departure but luckily we took Tony's advice and left two hours earlier. Tony had said Olympic Airways flights were always overbooked and the first people there had a chance of getting a seat. He was right. Our taxi driver was determined to set a new speed record to get us to the airport, presumably so he could fit in as many trips as possible. By this time we were used to Athens traffic and drivers so we did what all Greeks did before a journey: crossed ourselves, and hoped. The queue at the check-in desk for the Olympic Airways flight to Melbourne stretched across the terminal so we were glad we got there early. The more astute travellers had arrived three hours before the check-in time. Our first adventure with the airline was getting seats together. Despite booking as a couple we were issued with seats well away from each other. We stood our ground and after being told the plane was booked out and a bit of stern language in both Greek and English – my Greek language lessons of twenty years before helped – we were reluctantly seated together. Once on board we observed that many of the hostesses spent a lot of time at the back of the plane talking and smoking (which was allowed in those days) while two male stewards did most of the work. A Greek passenger seated next to us explained that the hostesses, now in their forties, had been personally hired by Onassis, the then owner of the airline, with stories of glamour being an air hostess. Onassis had since departed but they were left there in a very unglamorous job of looking after economy passengers, hence the uninterest and some bitterness.

At dinner time the meal was served. Mine was quite all right but Rob's was frozen solid inside and out. We eventually attracted a steward who took it away and eventually returned with the container just about too hot to handle but the inside still frozen solid. This was pointed out on our second call for sustenance and again the steward disappeared. This time he returned with a quite edible vegetarian meal, a leftover from the business class section. I am happy to say the rest of the flight, apart from being long and boring, was uneventful, the way I like airline flights.

FIFTEEN

Back to the Real World

My long-service leave was over so it was back to work at the ABC, getting the house and finances in order, and reintroducing ourselves to our two pet cats who had been spoilt rotten by the cattery where they had spent their long-service leave. During that time my friend John Liston, whom I had met in Ireland twenty years before and who I had kept in contact with, said he was coming to Australia to meet his brother. He wondered if I could show him the outback in January next year, 1988. His farm, near Tralee, was frozen over and he could get away for a month. I explained to him that outback Australia in January was quite the opposite and was very hot, but I would do what I could. I worked out that the best I could do with the time available, and without flying, was to drive up to the far west of New South Wales and head to south-west Queensland.

John duly arrived in Australia and after a visit to Sydney, he and I left Melbourne in the Toyota Corona on 5 January. Our destination was Tibooburra in the 'corner country' of north-west New South Wales. After several days of driving we got as far as Milparinka to be told that the roads were closed beyond Tibooburra because of tropical wet season rains, so going further north was out of the question. This meant travelling east to Wanaaring from where we could get to Bourke. I asked the local policeman at Milparinka what the track was like to Wanaaring. He asked me what I was driving and I said a Toyota Corona. He replied, 'That's OK, you'll get through.' I noticed he had a high base four-wheel drive Toyota Land Cruiser. He said not to worry. Parts of the track were under water but he had just driven back from there that morning and where the road was under water we could follow his tracks through the bush. So we started off and sure enough the track disappeared under water but I could see the track made by the police vehicle and the squashed bush, and so I followed them. At one stage I was led astray by some older tracks but luckily realised I had made a mistake and retraced my tyre marks to the police tracks. By early afternoon the temperature was around the 36°C mark and John was starting to realise that when I said January was going to be hot, it was hot. I had all the 'air-conditioning' in the Toyota working. All the windows were open and the air blower was going at full blast. Unfortunately our land speed was not great so not too much air movement was being created. We made it to Wanaaring with the car's undercarriage scrubbed clean. The police tracks took us along the right path and the track itself, or the sections not under water, were fairly easy to handle. The worst section was the remaining few kilometres of gravel road which had parts washed away by the recent rain.

We stayed overnight in a donga at the Wanaaring Hotel with John looking for relief in the 'cool' of the evening. Well, it did cool down to about 32°C overnight. The following morning John surrendered, and admitted that outback Australia in January was best avoided. As I had a few days to spare I thought the best place I could take my Irish visitor was to the Snowy Mountains.

So instead of north we headed south, showing off the sights of Cooma, Mount Kosciusko National Park, Jindabyne and Omeo – not the outback but a lot cooler.

Hotel and main street, Wanaaring, January 1988

In October, Expo 88 was being held in Brisbane and both Rob and I were able to co-ordinate holidays to spend a week at the exposition. By now we had car travel down to a fine art with each taking two-hour shifts in the driver's seat while the other navigated. Where possible we prebooked our accommodation which meant less hassle after a day's travelling. The trip was uneventful, going to Brisbane through the central west of New South Wales and returning via Sydney, Canberra and the Kosciusko National Park and once again returning to Melbourne through Suggan Buggan which thirty years before was just a two-wheel bush track but was now a fairly respectable gravel road.

Travelling at ground level was curtailed somewhat in 1990 although I did manage to get several weekend cycle trips in including one that introduced me to the ferocious leeches of South Gippsland in the Tarra–Bulga National Park on the Grand Ridge Road. I again took to the air, this time courtesy of the ABC. I was asked to train journalists to use a new computer programming system designed to handle radio and television news bulletins. Any job that got me travelling was very welcome. My first stint was in Sydney where I spent a couple of weeks. The training was carried out in the old ABC studios in Kings Cross where I unexpectedly was introduced to the delights of this cosmopolitan suburb. One day, waiting for the start of a class, I strolled to the window and looked across William Street. Opposite, on a first-floor balcony several young ladies, whom I suspect had worked long and hard during the night, had come out for a breath of fresh air and sunshine sans clothes, giving me a very good view for which the punters the previous night may have paid quite good money.

In Perth I admired the way they had got over the problem of trying to remember a security code to open a back door to the television studios; the code number was written above the key pad. Bunbury was one of the few places I have ever had a parking ticket. I was driving an ABC car at the time, so the parking ticket went to the Perth office but in good bureaucratic style eventually found its way to me in East Hawthorn. I surrendered meekly and sent the Bunbury City Council a cheque for $10.

The following year, 1991, there were more computer training visits. The one in Hobart was held in August. I can think of better months to work in Hobart, but I did have my revenge on my boss who organised the timetable. He came across to see how progress was going and we had just visited the television studios. Returning to the ABC radio studios, I suggested we walk since it was only a short distance. He had just flown from a 20°C day in Canberra and as we stepped onto the footpath the snow was falling.

After some training sessions in Launceston and Burnie, my work in Tasmania was completed and I flew back to Melbourne from the northern Tasmanian airport of Wynyard. While waiting for the flight, I was waylaid by the only other passenger, who was on a mission to convert the world to Christianity. I escaped his earnest attempts to save my soul from I'm not sure what, because when the twelve-seat plane landed, his seat was near the front and mine was near the back. Someone was watching over me. As we headed north there was a most ferocious-looking cloudbank looming up in front of us. Not being an expert on weather conditions, I was relieved when the pilot flew under the cloudbank and not into it or over it. We landed safely at Moorabbin airport in the south east of Melbourne.

Despite all the air travel I was looking forward to once again driving across to Perth as Rob had not yet gone further west than Adelaide. This time the Toyota took us along the coast as far as the Murray River. This included passing through Kingston South East and giving Rob the chance to admire the giant lobster. We bypassed Adelaide and revisited the Clare wine area before cutting across to Port Augusta. We took in the Eyre Peninsula, getting close and personal at the seal colony on Point Labatt, the only such colony on mainland Australia. We then headed west getting as far as Ceduna for an unscheduled two-night stop.

The next morning after the first night there we checked the car's radiator to find it bone dry. We put some water into it, which ran out at about the same rate. We were directed to a garage a short distance away which specialised in radiators for interstate trucks. If we had a Kenilworth or Mack or similar the old radiator

Giant lobster, Kingston South East, November 1991

would have been taken out and a new one dropped in straight away. No such provision was made for Toyota Coronas. The first question was how we were paying for it and I said, 'Cash.' That was the right answer, because we were told we would have to stay overnight but the car would be ready the following morning. The garage proprietor said he would arrange for a new radiator to be delivered from Adelaide overnight and it wouldn't take long to replace the old one.

After working and travelling through the outback I had learnt that unless you are well known, no local business will take cheques, you may or may not get away using credit cards away from places like hotels and motels, but cash is accepted everywhere. Before we left Rob had queried why I was putting $1000 in notes under the mat in the back seat of the car. He now knows why. We picked up the car, $400 went into the back pocket of the garage man, we got a hand-written receipt and off we went, all happy.

We had booked some accommodation but not at every point so we had some leeway in making up time. This did mean driving in the twilight west from Ceduna. I explained to Rob I would be travelling with only the parking lights on because of the danger from kangaroos at this time of night. We did see a couple of big ones near the road but they ignored us. I did not have a crash bar on the front of the Toyota, unlike the Renault. At the border town of Eucla, Rob was driving and I warned him that he would be stopped by the highway police and accused of speeding. As predicted we were and Rob looked suitably affronted as he showed them his licence. He was told to continue but watch his speed.

After admiring the wildflowers in Western Australia's south west, we arrived in Kalgoorlie where I was able to introduce Rob to the rules of two-up. He was a good learner and we both left $20 richer. We ended the journey in Perth and did the tourist bit which included a day visit to Rottnest Island. We then drove to East Perth station, put the car on the Indian Pacific train, found our compartment, and unexpectedly ran into a friend of ours who had a compartment to himself along with a case of sparkling wine to sustain him on the journey to Sydney. We were delighted to share his largesse. At Cook, where the train stops for half an hour, we checked the car. It was still where it should be and we took the obligatory photograph to prove it for future generations. We left the train at Adelaide, and recovered the car now well and truly covered in dust thrown up during the train trip. We had a long but uneventful drive back to Melbourne, all in one day.

The following year I was tied up with a job with the ABC in Sydney and more computer training in the Northern Territory. Again there was a plethora of air travel and testing trials with taxi drivers who either didn't know where you were going or wanted

Indian Pacific train with Toyota, Rob and friend, Cook, December 1991

to go a more advantageous way as far as they were concerned. I have often wondered how overseas travellers dealt with taxi drivers in Sydney or Melbourne who, for one reason or another, were geographically illiterate. The remaining computer training sessions for the ABC were in the Northern Territory, this time in October. Again, not the ideal time to visit the far north. These were followed by training at some regional stations around Victoria. The next question was what was next on the ABC's agenda. The answer was very little as far as travelling and teaching was concerned. The result was I had a good heart-to-heart talk with my accountant who then declared I had enough money in superannuation and investments to call it quits. I did, beginning the letter of retirement to the news editor at the time with: 'This is the first and last letter of this type I have ever written or will write again, I am retiring.' The date was 30 July 1993.

SIXTEEN

A Man of Leisure

Now that I was no longer a slave to the roster or the clock, what
better time to have a look at some of the remote places in Australia
that I had not yet ventured to with the Toyota. I even obtained a
permit to travel through some of the indigenous lands of Central
Australia. All to no avail. About a week or two after saying goodbye
to the ABC I received a phone call from the managing director of
the company that had been installing the new computer system
for the ABC News. His company was installing similar systems in
other newsrooms in Australia and south-east Asia. I had met him
many times while working for the ABC. He told me his permanent
trainer had resigned, and he didn't want another full-time trainer
but someone willing to travel and teach people as the need arose. I
said I was interested, so we talked about fees, payments and travel
arrangements. The minute I said 'Yes', he said, 'Good, you're
booked on a flight to Hong Kong leaving in October.' I suspect he
knew all along that I would accept the offer. Rob was also able to
come with me. The accommodation arranged for me was a hotel
room, and it did not matter how many people stayed in the room,
but Rob had to pay his own airfare. We made arrangements to drive
to Sydney, parking the Toyota in a spare garage at a friend's place

and flying from Sydney. Once again we took the picturesque but slow route through the Victorian Alps and the Kosciusko National Park. Again the Toyota proved its versatility as a mountain goat on the narrow roads and steep climbs. We took a leisurely three days to do the trip and duly parked the car in the spare garage.

We had no problem landing in Hong Kong and being driven to our hotel, but we did run into a slight language misunderstanding there. As we were staying for three weeks we asked that the mini-bar in the refrigerator in the room be emptied. The obliging staff then started to remove the whole unit until we explained it was only the contents and not the refrigerator itself that we wanted cleared. I spent the day teaching, which was interesting but fairly heavy going. For most pupils English was their second language or in some cases their third. There was also the problem of those students who had learnt their English from an American teacher. I found that at times American and Australian English are only vaguely related. It meant that at the end of the day I needed a strong drink. That was Rob's first job, to make sure one was waiting for me. As he had the day to himself to enjoy the versatility of Hong Kong he also had to find a restaurant for dinner. He did a good job of that, resulting in some interesting and enjoyable meals in some little cafes tucked away in side streets far from the big ones looking after the tourist dollar. He also had the task of looking after the laundry. He found the place which did the hotel's laundry and we had ours done for substantially less than if we had left it with the hotel.

I had the weekends off. On the second weekend I had free, we took the high-speed ferry from Hong Kong to the then Portuguese colony of Macau which takes about an hour. We did the tourist bit, discovering we could not bring a camera into one of the casinos for which Macau is well known. We did find a little family-run restaurant which served African chicken done the Portuguese way. On top of that were some very good Portuguese wines costing us the equivalent of A$15. In Hong Kong taxes on wine made it a luxury item. We had a very good lunch.

Eventually the television station staff I was training became computer literate and the job ended. During the training I became familiar with the Hong Kong train system, its efficiency and reliability. A company bus transported us from the railway station to the fairly isolated studios and back. The station was in the hills in the north-east of the then colony. I was reminded of home when I watched the plane with the kangaroo on the tail landing at the old Kai Tek airport. The kangaroo was visible between the residential towers as it flew low in over the city to the airport.

We had made arrangements to return to Australia via Thailand. We landed in Bangkok, taking a day or two to get used to the crowds, the traffic and the humidity. We also developed some athletic skill in using the water buses which pulled into piers for the briefest of time as you either leapt aboard or leapt off. Seeing the polluted state of the river was a great incentive not to misjudge your step. After having a look at Bangkok we took the overnight train to Chang Mai in the north. On boarding the train we were shown to the carriage and our bunks. The bunks were one above the other and parallel with the aisle. There were another two bunks opposite, and so on down the length of the carriage. Privacy came from a curtain drawn across once you found room for yourself and the luggage. You brought along your own bottles of water and occasionally a vendor would come along the carriage with fruit or some locally cooked food. On returning to Australia we queried the difference about what we had been told about the train and the actuality. We should have been on the first-class overnight train, and not, due to a booking mistake, on the economy version.

After the planned sightseeing around Chang Mai we returned to Bangkok on the daytime bus so we could see the country. At the scheduled time the hotel informed us our transport had arrived to take us to Bangkok. A rather well-used utility waited for us, and we were invited to get into the back in the open air. This looked like another novel way of travelling. However, we ended up at the bus station on the edge of town where a modern double-decker bus was waiting. The bus was too big to go through the narrow streets of Chang Mai hence the utility pickup. We chose the two front seats on the top section of the bus above the driver. This gave us a very good view of the road and countryside, and the traffic on the road. As the journey began and we observed the chaotic and suicidal traffic we were starting to doubt the wisdom of the choice. It also explained why there was no rush for the other front seats, especially when our driver drove around an oxen and cart plodding along the main highway without slowing down, while we appeared to be heading straight towards a large truck coming the other way. With centimetres to spare our bus got back to where it should be and the truck rushed past. After each near miss a certain immunity to danger developed and we started to admire the scenery and left our fate in the hands of the driver.

At around midday we stopped for lunch at a roadside café. Since arriving in Thailand we had eaten at the tourist hotels where the meals were Thai but Westernised to what they thought the visitors wanted. At the roadside cafe it was real homemade food served for the locals. It was different and a pleasant surprise. On arriving in Bangkok again the bus didn't attempt to navigate the city streets so a taxi transported us to the hotel. Happily, the flight from Bangkok to Sydney was uneventful but both Thai and Australian customs officials made us well aware of the dangers of carrying drugs or other illegal materials. Our car was patiently waiting for us and we gave it a good workout by driving straight from Sydney to Melbourne in one day.

My next training session overseas came the next year. The destination was Kuala Lumpur, Malaysia, where I had to train the staff of the national television and radio broadcasting service. Once again Rob came along for the ride and to provide the necessary nerve tonic at the end of each day as well as organising the dining experience and managing the laundry. We had personal contacts in Kuala Lumpur, local people who had been working in Melbourne, and we caught up with them. They introduced us to durians, a local edible fruit which has a very obnoxious odour but delicious pulp. Someone described it as like eating strawberries and cream in a dirty well-used lavatory. When we first arrived we saw notices in hotels saying 'No Durian Allowed' and we wondered who were these poor people who were being banned. It was too early in the season for local durians but we did try some imported from Thailand at a roadside stall during a tropical downpour. I really enjoyed the taste, and in the open the smell wasn't too bad.

One weekend our friends, who ran a small transport business, took us to the old coastal town of Melaka for a day trip. There is a tolled highway between Kuala Lumpur and Melaka. On the return journey we were caught up in a major traffic jam. We crawled along for several hours until we passed the cause of the problem, a major accident involving several vehicles. As soon as we were clear, our driver made up time by travelling well above the legal speed limit. I asked him about being booked for speeding. He said there was no problem as when you entered the tollway the time you passed through was noted and printed on your ticket. When you left the tollway and paid your money, the time you left was also noted and if you had travelled the distance in less time than the prescribed speed limit allowed, you got booked. In our case because of the holdup it didn't matter how fast we went because our tollway ticket showed we had kept well within the speed limit. At the end of the tollway the driver pointed out several motorcycle policemen waiting for a signal from the tollgate operator to book any motorist who had travelled too fast. Incidentally I did notice our driver reached 160 km/h which had been the fastest I had travelled on a road.

The training ended in Kuala Lumpur but while I was there another training job turned up in Hong Kong so once again both of us were back in familiar territory. We were in the same hotel, so sorting out the mini-bar was easier and Rob found the same laundry lady and several of our favourite restaurants. On the first spare weekend we took the fast ferry again to Macau and found the little restaurant with the African chicken on its menu and the good but very cheap Portuguese wine. Wine in Malaysia, like in Hong Kong, attracts very heavy taxes so we were more than pleased to make up a bit of lost time with the Portuguese vintages. Possibly we did make a bit too much of the opportunity: we managed to make the ferry back all right but I found it a little difficult putting pen to paper to fill in the immigration form to enter Hong Kong. The Customs let us in; perhaps it was not the first form they have attempted to decipher after someone has enjoyed the wines of Portugal in Macau.

During the second weekend break in Hong Kong we visited the New Territories, a district close to the Chinese border. There we travelled on the new tram system, noting that the trams had been made by Comag Engineering in Dandenong near Melbourne. It was good to see Australian expertise being exported. Eventually another Hong Kong broadcaster's newsroom was computer literate so we flew back to less polluted Melbourne.

On return we said goodbye to the faithful but now ten-year-old Toyota Corona and replaced it with a Honda Accord. Like the Toyota it was a manual-geared car which I found more reliable when the going gets tough and less to go wrong when you're hundreds of kilometres from the nearest garage. Being now happily retired, we made the Honda earn its keep with visits to various places in Victoria, including Rutherglen where we tested its carrying capacity with several full wine boxes. The Honda also showed it was capable of handling some difficult terrain when Rob and I had a holiday in Merimbula in southern New South Wales. Naturally we ignored the main highways and made our way there through the Victorian high country to Corryong and once again down the Geehi Walls trail on a much improved road to Thredbo, Jindabyne and the Kosciusko National Park. One short cut somewhere west of Pambula marked on the map as a dotted line turned out to be a fire track designed for fire-fighting four-wheel drive trucks, but the Honda survived unscathed despite some rough stones and steep grades.

After we settled into our serviced apartment in Merimbula, I had the opportunity to test the speed of the new car. Between Merimbula and Tathra just to the north, there is a stretch of road with no crossroads that goes down a valley and then slowly rises up the other side, giving a very clear view. On reaching 180 km/h I decided that was the fastest one could travel under ideal conditions as the aerodynamics caused by the speed began to lift the vehicle, making it slightly unstable. My theory is that modern vehicles unless purposely adapted for racing are too light for the speed their engines can produce, and very unsafe for poor drivers. After sampling the oysters and seafood of the area including some fish I was able to catch from the rocky shore of Ben Boyd National Park, we returned home the conventional way along the Princes Highway.

SEVENTEEN

The South Pacific Calls

Our next visit overseas was unassisted by commercial interests. We paid our own way for a holiday in Fiji flying from Melbourne to Nadi, Fiji's international airport, on an Air Canada plane loaned to Qantas for some reason as we had booked through Qantas. We had arranged transport from Nadi on one side of the main island to Suva on the other side. We expected a bus to take us there along with other passengers. Instead a Fijian of Indian descent was waiting with his Mercedes-Benz to take just the two of us to our motel in Suva. He also owned a sugar plantation. On the way he asked if we minded if he called in to see his wife and family before the children headed for school. We agreed, and on arrival at the farm we were invited into his house. We met his family and were given a very nice cup of coffee and some small cakes before being driven on to Suva. It was quite unexpected, and it was such a warm and friendly greeting into the country.

We took the opportunity to take a few organised day tours including one that took us to a luxury tourist resort on the coast. Some people may enjoy this type of holiday but to me the resort was too isolated and unless you organised a taxi or a tour, there was no chance to walk around a local village or town and meet the local people. Our motel in Suva gave us the chance to wander to the shops, markets and local cafes, and learn more about the community. We hired a car to drive around the main island, Vita Levu. The centre of the island is quite mountainous so the road skirts around the coastline. In parts the road was a bit challenging but in other parts quite good, especially between some of the main centres. It was not a difficult drive but definitely not designed for speed. We did the whole island in a day including the compulsory photo stops. We handed back the hire car unscathed although I can't vouch for the suspension. We spent the next few days again having a look around Suva before heading home.

Road and rocky outcrops, Fiji, June 1995

We had booked on a local airline to fly from Suva to the international airport in Nadi. The flight would take us across the mountainous centre of Vita Levu, which we hadn't had a chance to see on our car trip. We planned to arrive just a short time before the flight was due to leave. Luckily we took the advice of the motel receptionist to get there early because these flights were always overbooked. The receptionist was right. The plane took 12 passengers and 14 passengers turned up. By the way the staff at the check-in counter reacted, this was not an unusual occurrence. Rob and I were eventually allocated seats but two very distressed Australians were left in the terminal as we took off. There was no problem at Nadi, where we got our seats in a real Qantas plane and arrived safely back to Melbourne. Going through Customs we declared our wooden carving and followed the red line to the agriculture quarantine area where our purchases were checked and approved, allowing us a quick departure from the terminal.

Back on home soil it didn't take long to pack the Honda and take Rob to my old stamping ground in south-west Queensland and show him some of the outback he hadn't seen. This included a visit to the Mungo National Park that includes the dried-up Lake Mungo. In the Dreamtime it was very popular because it was filled with water and surrounded by scrub and many animals. It was a great food bowl for those Australians thousands of years ago.

Over the next few days we made our way once again using the Wilcannia to Bourke road along the Darling River, and I was happy to say they had rebuilt the hotel at Louth halfway in between, with once again cold beer on tap. In Bourke I noticed a small change in the town. Many of the shops had protective wire screens across their windows giving the place the appearance of being under siege, although our night there was peaceful.

The roads now were of a much higher standard than when I worked at Charleville 35 years before so driving was much easier. The town itself had not changed very much over those years although the motel we stayed in was new. Corones, the big pub

The main street, Louth, October 1995

in the centre of the town, was now legally serving beer after ten o'clock. From Charleville we drove east along the highway, now bitumen with bridges and culverts, to Toowoomba and the Gold Coast, the corrugations, gravel and steep little creek crossings just a memory of the past. We had a pleasant week-long break in the Gold Coast catching up with old friends. Driving south along the coast to Sydney we found the ferries across the Clarence and other rivers had now been replaced by new concrete bridges. From Sydney our route took us along the Olympic Way and Hume Highway to home.

By now, 1996, the train line to Darwin had been built. My cycling companion on my ride to Sydney fifteen years ago, Graeme Parker, now retired, suggested we try out the Ghan train from Adelaide to Darwin. We started off with the Overland Express, the old one which travelled overnight on the broad gauge via

Ballarat. Then we boarded the Ghan and relaxed as we were fed and watered all the way to Darwin. Train travel is great. We made use of the lounge car, watched the world go by, were well fed in the dining car and the bar was always open. What is entertaining is meeting fellow travellers from around the world. They are all different but they have one thing in common, the desire to get out, see the world and meet other people. There's no point in being shy when travelling.

We took to the sky to get from Darwin to Cairns but not before there was a mix-up at the check-in counter, where I was upgraded to business class and my companion was left travelling in economy. I am not sure yet if Qantas has been forgiven. There were no further travel upsets as we took the Queenslander train to Brisbane, which was the first-class edition of the Sunlander. After again being well fed and watered, we took to the skies, this time together, to fly home to Melbourne.

While I had been gallivanting around north and eastern Australia Rob had stayed home, looking after the cats and keeping the house in order. It was his turn and so once again the Honda was loaded up and we headed west. He had planned a week's stay on board the paddle steamer the *Murray Princess*, based at Mannum in South Australia and plies between Swan Reach and Goolwa. Before this excursion we thought a week on Kangaroo Island would be a good start. This time we went the inland way to Mount Gambier by way of Ballarat, Hamilton and Casterton, and then along the coast to Victor Harbor and through the wine country of McLaren Vale to Cape Jervis where the vehicle ferry sails to Kangaroo Island.

We were advised to book the ferry trip, as it only runs once a day and if it is full that's your bad luck. Rob volunteered to drive onto the ferry thinking it was drive on, drive off. No, you back on and drive off as Rob discovered when he was directed to back into a tight corner so other vehicles could be fitted on. We admired the driver of a car towing a caravan who backed the caravan in with practiced ease. It was easy going at the other end. Once on the island we soon realised why people left the keys in their cars. The only way you were going to get off the island was on the one ferry each day, so why bother.

We stayed at the Ozone Hotel in Kingscote, the main settlement. The fishing was good nearby and on a couple of nights I was able to offer the hotel fresh fish in exchange for several being cooked for us. The seal that had taken up residence on a low platform at the end of the pier must have also realised fishing was good. I also located an uncle of mine whom I had not seen since I was a child. He was in a retirement home and his son, my cousin, was the only plumber on the island. My elderly uncle liked travel and was eager to come with us when we said we were going to drive to Cape Banda, the most westerly tip of the island. He said he had never been out there before. That apparent ignorance of the locality was soon dispelled when he started to point out various places and give us a running commentary on what we were seeing. He knew every inch of the way and he enjoyed the day out; good luck to him.

On leaving the island Rob was prepared to back on to the ferry and did it with aplomb. We arrived at Mannum on schedule, were able to park the car in a lockup shed and found our cabin on board the *Murray Princess*. Along with the other passengers we soon became adept at using gangplanks to go ashore when we tied up on the banks of the Murray for an overnight stay and occasional barbecue. On the way home we went directly east to Wentworth and stayed overnight in Moulamein at the same hotel we stayed in when we first met in 1971. From there we had a nostalgic look at Deniliquin before heading south to home.

Murray Princess *at Piggy Flat landing, September 1996*

The following year was a quiet one for travel. The only time the Honda really stretched its wheels was a trip to the Gold Coast. My two former ABC colleagues, Tony and Elaine Wilson, whom we had last seen in Greece, were managing the Tugun Hotel at Tugun and we were invited to stay for a few days. Who can turn down an offer of a week beside the beach? This time we drove more or less directly north from Melbourne which took us again into western New South Wales and by some now familiar towns as Parkes and Dubbo and less familiar ones as Goondiwindi and Warwick. It was one of those trips when everything worked out as planned. Certainly not boring, but nothing unexpected, and a good time was had by all. The return trip was again fairly direct using the Newell Highway. By then it had become a favourite route for truck transport which meant more concentration on the road and less leisurely sight-seeing.

An article in the *Australian Geographic* magazine intrigued Rob and me. It was a cruise on board a catamaran, *Coral Princess*, from Darwin to Broome visiting some of the remote parts of the Kimberley in northern Western Australia. It took only 48 passengers, so we booked to do this cruise in 1998. To come ashore at places where there was no wharf, a landing barge was used which could take all the passengers and two crew. Depending on the slope of the beach we were told whether we could step ashore from the barge onto dry land or had to wade through shallow water. Apart from the fantastic scenery, one of the first highlights was a pod of whales that circled and dived under the ship as we cruised through Admiralty Gulf shortly after leaving Darwin. I felt a certain amount of awe and apprehension as these giants of the ocean showed no concern for this strange craft. Soon after, this act was followed by two yellow sea snakes copulating in full view of the ship. Nature was certainly turning on a wonderful display.

One little bay we visited was a place where an opportunistic land salesman in Melbourne, on the other side of the continent, persuaded some investors that the particular area was a great place to farm sheep. This happened in the early nineteenth century. As far as scams go, nothing much has changed since. Incidentally, the local crocodiles made short work of the first and only flock of sheep to arrive. Another glimpse we had of early Australian history was at some local rock art where the first Australians drew pictures of the Dutch sailors in their uniforms who visited the coastline in the seventeenth century. One evening we moored near a pearl farm, which is heavily guarded. However, in the outback everyone helps each other, so in exchange for some sugar, of which the ship was running short, the workers at the farm received several slabs of beer.

Lagoon at Tranquil Bay, Kimberley coast, June 1998

On one of the coral islands we visited, we landed at low tide and were able to admire the pools and the coral contents but were told that at high tide the water would be two metres above the island. We were also able to visit the Mitchell Plateau with its spectacular waterfalls. It is some distance from the coast so the *Coral Princess* berthed near a small sandy beach from where helicopters flew us to the Plateau. We got a great view of this remarkable landscape from the helicopter and no one was concerned about the unorthodox landing platforms. We felt the pilots had done this before. Like all good things, the cruise came to an end at Broome. The following day we flew to Perth and were booked on board the red-eye special, the Qantas flight to Melbourne which leaves at one o'clock in the morning. Rob in his jovial manner asked the lady at the check-in desk for a seat near the pointy end of the plane. We learnt that there was no guarantee that people working on these desks have a sense of humour. We had the last two seats in economy at the tail end the plane, the furthest from the pointy end. We got home safely.

Explorer *and* Coral Princess, *Merazzi Bay, Kimberley coast, June 1998*

Ruins of settlement, Camden Harbour, Kimberley July 1998

Wading across Montgomery Reef, Kimberley, July 1998

EIGHTEEN

Around the World by Train and Air

We were saving money for 1998. My sister, Lynnette, who was living in England turned 60 that year so we decided to pop across to wish her a happy birthday. Of course the only way to travel was by train. The first obstacle was the amount of water between Australia and Singapore so we had to look to Qantas to get us there, which it duly did. We had also upgraded our air travel from economy to business class. The experience of sitting at the back of the red-eye special from Perth, and age, made me think more of comfort and less about the bank balance. After a short spell in Singapore we began our train journey to England. The first leg was aboard the Eastern Orient Express, a tourist train that travelled between Singapore and Bangkok. In its first life it was the Silver Fern Express which plied between Wellington and Auckland in New Zealand. It had been transformed into a first-class train with lounge and dining cars and the observation platform at the bank of the train. Impeccably dressed, we had no problem going through Malaysian customs at the railway station – no baggy shorts this time. There was definitely a difference between our tourist train and the commuter train we first used years earlier. As part of the journey the train took a branch line to Kanchanaburi for a brief stop near the infamous bridge over the River Kwai and the 'death railway' constructed during World War II. The conquering Japanese used captured Australian and Allied prisoners and local people to build a railway to Burma, using extreme cruelty and torture. There was a sombre visit by bus to an Allied war cemetery and on the way our courier told us we may see an elephant being washed in a nearby river. The elephant and keeper were there right on cue. At the small station of Kanchanaburi we had to walk through a local train to reach our train. There was quite a contrast in elegance and style.

Eastern Orient Express and countryside, Central Malaysia, September 1998

Once again we experienced the noise, bustle and smells of Bangkok before being whisked by air to Rome by the flying kangaroo. We admired the Italian railway system as a fast train took us straight from the airport 50 kilometres from the centre of Rome to the main station right in the heart of the city. With the experience of Australian taxi drivers at the back of our mind, we apprehensively took a taxi to our hotel right near the old Roman centre. On arrival at the hotel after a lot of twists and turns in our journey we checked our city map and, taking into account the number of one-way streets, the taxi driver had taken us the shortest way possible. A plus mark for Rome's taxi drivers.

Before we left Australia, we bought an Italian rail pass which allowed us to travel first class, but not on two consecutive days, which worked out well. We also worked out the public transport in Rome and got a four-day pass which again was a great way of seeing the city. There was one exception; we took a bus through a hilly suburb towards Vatican City. The problem was, on one of the smaller roads there had been a landslide and the bus terminated there. We had to stay with the bus while it carefully turned around and returned to the start. We picked up another bus to get us to the centre of the Roman Catholic empire. On this day, much to Rob's annoyance, the façade of Saint Peter's Basilica was hidden behind scaffolding as maintenance was being carried out. The Sistine Chapel was also a bit of a shock. The roof paintings were magnificent but any sense of spiritual dignity or reverence was lost in the noise and bustle of hundreds of tourists crowding into the small area. When we visited the Coliseum we walked around the historic arena and were met by a variety of cats, some friendly, others suspicious. We were told that this was their regular home.

From Rome we travelled to Florence with its plethora of Davids. We did see the real one in a museum. Many Italians have relatives in Australia as I found out the first time I visited the country. We noticed a toy koala on the outside doorpost on a house in the hilly suburb of Fiesole. Our next train stop was Pisa and we found we had been booked into a tourist hotel at

San Giuliano some 15 kilometres from Pisa. We decided not to eat in the hotel restaurant that night but instead walked to the centre of the village and found a little family-run restaurant with good Italian food and their own wine which they sold to us at the equivalent of A$1.00 a litre. The next day we took the local bus into Pisa for the tourist bit. This time we were unable to climb the leaning tower and had to admire it from a distance noting the heavy earthworks used to prop it up.

The following day we had to get the train to Genoa from Pisa station. We decided we couldn't use the local bus service to get to Pisa from San Giuliano as there was not enough room for luggage. There was a branch railway line from goodness knows where to Pisa which passed through San Giuliano. I went to the local station and found that a train could get us and our luggage to Pisa in time to catch our train to Genoa. Sure enough on schedule the warning signals on the nearby road began to operate and into view came a well-used diesel railcar and carriage belching out more black smoke than any steam engine, grinding, literally, to a halt at the station. The two of us and a local lady clambered aboard, the conductor acknowledged our rail passes and we rattled onto Pisa.

A much more modern and comfortable train was waiting to take us to Genoa with the railway line following the coast along a succession of tunnels and viaducts and seaside towns. A very scenic journey, and a good reason for using the train. Walking from the station to the nearby hotel Rob, who was following me, was accosted by a group of gypsies asking for money in a rather threatening way. A not too uncommon occurrence. I don't know how good their English was but they certainly understood the Australian request put strongly to 'get fumigated' or something like that. Happily, Rob did not lose any possessions in the

Koala on a house in Fiesole, Florence, September 1998

encounter. Otherwise our tourist visit to this picturesque seaport was uneventful.

A quick train trip took us from the port city to inland Milan. Due to our appreciation of cheese we knew Milan was the home of the Gorgonzola variety. Gorgonzola was the village from where the cheese originated. We took a suburban train to Gorgonzola and from the station all we could see were high rise flats stretching into the distance and not a cow or blade of grass in sight. At the station there was a small statue of a cow proclaiming this was where the Gorgonzola cheese was born.

Apartments at Gorgonzola, the original village
famous for its cheeses, September 1998

We travelled east across northern Italy with a stop at Bologna where the very comfortable hotel was uncomfortably close to a narrow alley favoured by drug dealers and users. I suspect every city has these places. To us, the casual tourists, there were no signs of these problems when we arrived in Venice. We soon learnt the skill of using the water bus service which provided an invaluable public transport service. Like Bangkok, the thought of landing in the canal was enough to make sure we had a firm grip and took a quick and accurate step on or off.

The next stage in our rail trip was on board the Orient Express from Venice to the French port of Boulogne. I regarded the Orient Express as a museum on wheels. The carriages have been restored after the ravages of World War II, or in some cases rebuilt. The interior has been restored to what it was in the train's heyday in the 1930s with magnificent wooden panelling and windows that open. No air-conditioning, and heating in every compartment came from heaters warmed by water from boilers at the end of each carriage. We boarded the train at Venice and the first thing we noticed were the little curls of smoke coming out of the boiler

Cliff beside the Orient Express, Innsbruck, Austria September 1998

chimneys at the end of each carriage. Our cabin had two bunks, and a washbasin. The toilets were at each end of the carriage and there were no showers or shared bathroom. I speculated what conditions would have been like in the 1920s and 1930s on the original train as it steamed across Europe at the height of summer, taking four or five days to travel between Paris and Istanbul. The one concession to modern travel was the high speed bogies on the carriages and the powerful diesel electric engines enabling the train to travel at the high speeds required on main line railways.

The highlight of this one night and two days trip was the dinner on board the Orient Express. We were told when we booked for the journey that gentlemen were requested to wear dinner jackets and ties for the dinner and ladies evening gowns. As we were from the antipodes, Rob and I settled for black reefer jackets and grey trousers. This was accepted in the dining car. The food was excellent and the wine list was also of the same high standard and was priced accordingly. I said to Rob we were having a bottle of wine with this meal even if we had to mortgage the house to pay for it! We also noted that the ladies did dress up magnificently for the occasion and if the jewellery they were wearing was genuine it could have been used to pay off the debt of a third-world country. Two ladies we met that night had flown from England to Venice specially to have dinner on board the Orient Express. I don't think they would have been disappointed.

Our journey ended the following afternoon at the French port of Boulogne. There a channel ferry took us across to the English port of Falmouth where we boarded the Brighton Belle train, again an historic train restored to its original splendour and was part of the tour. On boarding we were served scones, cream and strawberry jam along with champagne. Our brief visit back in time to the world of luxury train travel ended with a realistic thud as we as we arrived at Liverpool Street station in London right at the start of peak hour. We had to get a tube train to Paddington to get our train to Reading. To start with Rob wanted to go to the toilet and found you had to pay to get in and of course we had no English coins. That took a bit of sorting out. Then we crammed aboard a well-filled tube train along with our cases to get to Paddington.

There I had a British railways pass that had to be validated. We could not do this at the ticket counter but had to go to the information desk manned by an Indian gentleman with a beard and wearing Sikh headgear. He could have been an extra from a BBC English comedy. I left Rob looking after the luggage while I tried to get this pass stamped. An hour and a half later I returned with the valid tickets to a very concerned Rob who had wondered what had happened to me. What did happen was that at the head of the queue was a woman who was trying to get the cheapest possible journey from one town to another and wanted to know every option available. Each one depended on the time of travel and the type of train. Eventually she chose the one she wanted and then when asked to pay produced a string of credit cards. After about the fifth try one card did actually have some money on it. Eventually it was my turn to arrive at the window and within a minute I had the appropriate stamp on the pass and was able to travel.

We got the next train to Reading where a very patient sister was waiting to pick us up and take us to her house. I told her the story of the ticket saga and she was not surprised. Lynnette had arranged a number of trips to show us around and these included some visits to historic homes as she was a member of the National Trust. One day trip was across to the Isle of Wight where I enjoyed a trip on a little tourist railway that was running on the remnants of a rail network that once serviced the island. Lynnette's dog that had accompanied us just about had a nervous breakdown as the steam engine expelled a blast of steam right near him.

Rob left us briefly to visit other friends in England and I accepted my sister's offer of driving to France for lunch. She had bought shares in the English Chunnel project but the only dividend she got was a once-a-year pass to use the Chunnel. So along with two of her friends we drove to Dover where we and the car went on to a flat-top carriage on the train which took us under the English Channel. The journey took half an hour but before boarding we had to go through French customs which was quick and efficient. At Calais in France we followed the white lines that had us driving on the right-hand side of the road. Lynnette had done this before and appeared relaxed and I was given the task of navigating. I quickly found out one of the perils of being on the wrong side of the road. Reading my road map I instructed my sister to turn left at the next road, which she did automatically because in England like in Australia it is a simple exercise. In France we had to cut across oncoming traffic bringing a loud blast from the horn of a car coming the other way. Without further drama we found the little village with a good restaurant we were looking for and returned that evening to Reading without incident. We did call in at the duty-free liquor store at Calais, which apparently was mandatory for English visitors, and with four in the car we could return with an ample and legal supply of alcoholic goodies.

On 8 October 1988 we duly celebrated my sister's sixtieth birthday with roast beef and all that went with it in true English style. Mission accomplished, we headed home, this time by air. Our first stop was San Francisco where we did the tourist thing

Restaurant and shops, Montreuil, France, October 1998

and queued for an hour to board one of their famous cable cars just to say we had done it. Getting around otherwise we used public transport, a very efficient bus and tram service. A tram line runs along Market Street, the main street. Many of the trams are historic and have come from other American cities where they had been removed. There were some from other countries including a Melbourne tram that had done its bit in Australia. Under the street was an underground tram service with more modern vehicles that we used to get to Ocean Beach on the Pacific Ocean. There were also new tram lines being laid down as the system was being expanded.

We broke the long flight home to Australia with a stopover in Honolulu that included a day tour of the main island. One stop was Sunset Beach known for its huge waves and international surf competitions. As luck would have it, there was hardly a ripple as wavelets gently lapped the sand. We crossed the International Date Line on the way back to Sydney and, like many other travellers, took a bit of time sorting out what day it was. The around-the-world trip ended on a domestic flight from Sydney to Melbourne.

After all that travel, a quiet time was spent at home where we reintroduced ourselves to our pet cats who had again been spoilt rotten at the cattery. With a plethora of frequent flyer points, a trip to Darwin was in order in March. There I was introduced to the pet horse at the Gove Hill hotel. A word of explanation: Gove Hill was a station on the now defunct Darwin to Birdum railway line. Gove Hill is at the southern edge of Kakadu National Park and not far from the mining town of Pine Creek. Friends of mine in Darwin had taken me for a two-day trip to Kakadu and were keen to show me Gove Hill hotel and how some of the rail infrastructure had been restored at the old railway yards. At the hotel we met the horse, a large white pony which had the habit of walking into the bar to meet visitors and was quite at home in this unusual stable. On returning to Melbourne we couldn't resist taking the Ghan train to Adelaide but used some excess frequent flyer points to get home.

We couldn't stay home for too long, so in October 1999 we proposed a drive around Tasmania. This time we did some planning and picked four places to stay and do short trips from the four centres. These were Launceston, Hobart, Queenstown and Somerset near Burnie. We left Melbourne the day after the motorcycle grand prix on Phillip Island in southern Victoria. As directed I parked the car on board the Bass Strait ferry, *Spirit of Tasmania*, and joined Rob in our cabin for the overnight trip. Next morning I went down to collect the car to find that the remainder of the car deck was filled with about one hundred

The horse at Grove Hill Heritage Hotel, March 1999

motorcycles. These were in front of the cars and had to leave first. The motorcyclists collected their machines and all of them started their engines for departure at about the same time. The noise was deafening inside the deck and I, along with the other car drivers, was glad to see the doors open and the cyclists ride off into the morning sun. It was a very noisy welcome to Devonport where the ferry berthed in Tasmania.

We mapped out a circuitous drive to Launceston, our first stopping place, and admired the way the major and minor roads in Tasmania were all labelled with numbers along with the destination signs. It made navigating much easier. Several years later the same system was introduced into Victoria. On one of the day trips to the north-east of the state Rob received a ticket for exceeding a school zone speed limit. These had yet to be introduced into Victoria and it was one of those days when police were conducting a blitz on this particular school. We explained we were unfamiliar with these new restrictions but to no avail so we paid the $100 fine at the next town, Derby, getting it out of the way. Near Gladstone, which is literally at the end of the road in the far north-east of the state, we went to a nearby lookout to get some photos of the area. Rob's mobile phone rang – no urgent message, just a call from a friend wanting to know how things were going. He was quite surprised to learn all was going well in northern Tasmania. The signal was excellent with no signs of any telephone towers. Sometimes modern technology really works. The next day we drove south-west from Launceston to Miena on Great Lake in the mountainous central plateau. At eleven o'clock on Saturday morning, on a remote gravel road, I was pulled over at a police roadblock for a breathalyser test. It was done by the same policeman who had booked Rob the previous day for going too fast through the school zone. He saw the humour in the situation but I still got breath tested, passing with flying colours. I did wonder that this remote location seemed an unusual place for testing one's alcohol level so early in the day. He explained that a lot of fishermen came up early for fishing on the lake. As it was up in the mountains some internal heating was occasionally required to thwart the cold. Hence the reminder that it was not a good idea to combine fishing, fighting the cold and driving.

Several days later we moved on to Hobart at a leisurely pace. With the narrow and at times very windy roads in the state it was the only way to travel. We had plenty to see and the Honda was doing its duty. Without incident we headed west to our next port of call, Queenstown. It was a much faster rate of travel than when, nearly fifty years before, I had hitchhiked through the area with the help of HEC trucks. As we approached Queenstown the devastation to the landscape through years of mining and the result of mineral processing was evident. The road descends into the town through what can be described as a moonscape of bare rocks and dirt. It was a formidable sight. I made a point of again visiting the local football oval. There was still no sign of grass, just a hard gravel surface. I still don't know if a visiting team has been able to win a match.

We included Strahan in one of our day trips in the area and learnt more of the horrors of the convict settlements on Sarah Island in Lake Macquarie. We also observed the fierce nature of the weather on the lake as a frightening squall cut visibility, shortening our trip on the tourist launch. The launch had intended to take us to the sea entrance to the lake called Hell's Gate, a formidable gap between two rugged cliffs. but as the rain blotted out the shoreline the captain decided passenger safety was the preferred option. Heading north for our final four-day break at Somerset we visited or, in my case, revisited Waratah where, as part of my last stay, I had been enrolled in the snooker tournament. The hotel and the remains of the tin mine dredge were still there, unchanged. The remainder of the visit was taken up with tourist duties, very enjoyable of course, and the drive back to Devonport for the cruise across Bass Strait on the ferry to Port Melbourne. Not a single motorcycle in the ship's hold.

Not too much travel was involved with the last year of the second millennium. Much of my time was working as a volunteer in Sydney for the Olympic Games and the Paralympic Games. I will confess I used air travel as the means of getting to and from Sydney. I think there were a number of frequent flyer points available to make use of this form of transport.

After the sporting dust had settled late in the year, Rob and I took a Steamrail four-day trip to Robinvale and back on trains pulled by 'K' and 'R' class steam locomotives. Steamrail is a volunteer organisation aimed at preserving Victoria's historic rail history centred around steam engine power. We travelled on some lines that are now only used by goods trains including the line to Robinvale. It was interesting to watch as the volunteers cleared debris from the rail turntable at Robinvale and got it into working order so that the two steam locomotives could be turned around. Those on the excursion had the option of paying extra for a sleeping berth or savour sleeping on carriage seats. The trains stopped overnight at Inglewood, Robinvale and Bridgewater, going to Robinvale via Ballarat and returning via Bendigo. For those old enough to remember, memories of snorting steam engines, open carriage windows, the smell of smoke and the clickety-clack of wheels along the tracks came flooding back.

'K' class locomotive on a turntable at Robinvale, June 2000

We ended the year by getting the Honda to take us to the Gold Coast where once again we met up with my two former colleagues, Tony and Elaine Wilson, who now had a home at Burleigh Heads. We headed north through one of the places I did call home at one stage, Deniliquin, and then through Hay with one overnight stop at Inverell in northern New South Wales. On the way to Inverell we admired the sleek beef cattle grazing in the area. We booked in at a motel and had dinner at a local club. With what we had seen during the day in mind, we thought that this would be an excellent time to sample the local product so we ordered steak. So much for what we saw in the paddocks. The steaks were so tough we could have replaced the tyres of the car with them and they would have shown no sign of wear by the time we reached the Gold Coast. Our stay at Burleigh Heads soon rid us of the memories of the Inverell experience. Just the opposite in fact. Returning home we avoided Sydney and made use of the quieter roads via Coonabarabran, Dubbo and Wagga Wagga.

NINETEEN

New Millennium – New Adventures

A new millennium dawned and as it neared the end of its first year we marked it by taking a bus and train tour of New Zealand organised by Grand Pacific Tours. We sat back and enjoyed the scenery as buses, launches and trains took us around the country. With some early starts, we soon understood why the tour leaders warned us that this was a tour, not a holiday, and it could involve some hard work. It was well worth it. On a small tourist railway that ran between Glenbrook and Waihi near Auckland, I had the opportunity to ride on the footplate of the steam engine. Our next train journey was from Taumarunui to Wellington on the Overlander, the regular commuter train between Auckland and Wellington. This time I was able to ride on the observation platform at the end of the last carriage.

When the British first settled in New Zealand they built a network of railways using the narrow or 'cape' gauge. This allowed railways to be built through narrow gorges and mountainous country, enabling people and supplies to reach remote farming and mining areas. As road transport superseded rail, many of these railway lines were closed but in some cases the value of tourism was recognised and some lines were restored. Major rail links between big towns remained open.

Taieri Express over Wingatui viaduct, New Zealand, November 2001

After safely being shown around the North Island, our tour group was ferried across Cook Strait to the South Island. Stepping off the ferry at Picton we went straight on board the train to Christchurch. The strait between North and South Islands has a bad reputation for storms. The day we travelled there wasn't even a passing breeze to disturb the tranquillity of the water. On the way to Christchurch there was one sight that was not listed on the brochures. Three teenagers on a beach near the railway line turned their backs on the train, dropped their trousers, bent over and gave us a rather unusual salute. Welcome to the South Island.

One of the most popular tourist railways runs from Dunedin in to the old mining settlements of Arthur's Knob and The Reefs. The group was amazed at the skill shown by the early engineers in building the railway. It clings its way along steep hills and gorges.

Powerful steam engines would have been needed to haul the loads of goods and people through this terrain. We met another group of railway enthusiasts who had restored one of the historic steam trains, the Kingston Flyer that connected the mining settlements around Queenstown to the outside world. Their story was that although they were able to keep the steam train going they did not have enough resources to restore the track and up to the time we were there they had had no help from the government despite the train's tourism value. As a result, the top speed of this famous train was 20 miles an hour, just a crawl compared to its speed when in full steam. I have heard that story before from similar volunteer organisations.

Kingston Flyer, Kingston, New Zealand, November 2001

Our bus took us through much of the South Island to the west coast where we ended on our last train of the tour, the Trans–Alpine train with connects Greymouth on the west coast with

Christchurch, winding its way across the Southern Alps; again, remarkable engineering through remarkable scenery providing a remarkable memory, and a spectacular end to a great trip. Then it was home by air from Christchurch to Melbourne.

As one approaches their use-by date, three score years and ten, the urge to travel continues, but the methods change and the idea of someone else doing the organising becomes more appealing. The result was that Rob and I took our first tour with Captain's Choice, a Melbourne-based travel agency which specialises in travel to more exotic destinations. Our choice was called the Silk Road tour which was advertised as following as near as possible the old Silk Road of Marco Polo fame in the middle ages, used for trade between China and Europe. The original travellers used camels and horses, but we were happy with two special trains complete with sleeping berths, lounge and dining cars; much more comfortable.

The first stage began from Beijing and we needed the airlines to get us there from Melbourne. The air part of the journey was uneventful although a world-wide influenza epidemic was making headlines and frightening off travellers. On the Hong Kong to Beijing flight we had the luxury of a practically empty business-class section with as many stewards as passengers.

With someone else doing the organising we were soon aboard the special train, the Chinese Orient Express, and heading west past the beginning of the Great Wall and of course the warriors of Xian. Travelling by rail takes you along the backs of houses and factories and the amount of rubbish strewn along the way attracted our attention, as did the smog. We were about 1500 kilometres west of Beijing before the air became clear of pollution caused by industry, cars and trucks. We marvelled at the way our

Chinese tour couriers ushered our group of about a hundred through the crowded railway stations and onto the right platform leading to our train. At one stop there was a fierce argument between our chief Chinese courier and a station official regarding boarding the train which just about led to blows. It was all about some regulation about the time of boarding although there was no logical reason for this to be followed to the letter. It was very similar to the attitude I had seen in the era of the bureaucratic Soviet Union.

The oddities of international trade emerged at Dunhuang in far western China where we stayed the night in a local hotel. We had travelled by bus from the nearest railway station to visit the historic town, incidentally seeing the end of the Great Wall on the way. They were just ruined remnants of this engineering feat. At dinner that night our courier provided us with some Australian wine found at the local supermarket costing only the equivalent

Chinese Orient Express at Dabancheng, April 2003

of $3.00 a bottle. There was no identification on the bottle except 'Wine of Australia'. How it got to western China at that cost is one of those deep mysteries of finance. The wine tasted quite good.

At the China–Kazakhstan border, we had another run-in with bureaucracy. Our train, on standard gauge, was able to cross the border to the first Kazakhstan station of Dostyk where the broad gauge system of the former Soviet Union began. However, at the Chinese border village of Dzungarian Gate, the authorities decreed that we were to leave the train and be taken by bus to Tacheng some 200 kilometres north, go through immigration there and be bussed to Dostyk to board our Russian train. It was an unfortunate time for this group of Australian travellers, who were at the wrong border at the wrong time. One day earlier Australia had supported the United States' invasion of Iraq which had annoyed the Chinese and Russians. We had been told diplomatic talks had gone as far as Beijing over the proposal to use the distant border crossing. Eventually we were able to cross at the Dzungarian Gate border. At this crossing there was actually a large immigration hall standing empty that local party officials had been trying to utilise for some time. Soon all had been sorted out and, guarded by a local, fully armed, militia unit, we were processed quickly and easily through the formalities and were soon back on the buses heading for Kazakhstan. As we left the centre the soldiers came out, formed a guard of honour and saluted as we drove off. The actual border, about a few hundred metres further on, was defined by a wire fence seen on any rural property and a sentry box with a lone soldier who waved the buses through.

At Dostyk we could see our waiting train, the Rus, at the station but some official somewhere had decreed we had to wait for someone's approval. Suddenly we were allowed to board and settle in to a very comfortable train that had been used to carry officials around in the time of the Soviets. As we travelled west along the old Silk Road route we passed through the recently independent republics of Kazakhstan, Krygyzstan, Uzbekistan and Turkmenistan before reaching the Russian Federation, all part of the old Soviet Union. The train only travelled about 50 kilometres through Krygyzstan. When the railways were built in the time of the Russian Empire these international borders did not exist.

Rus train at Tashkent, Uzbekistan, April 2003

These border crossing appeared to have been well organised by Captain's Choice, with most of the paper work being done between train staff and border officials in the club car that had the bar. For the passengers, highlights of the tour were visiting the historic towns along this old route and understanding its history. We were also introduced to a local sporting activity. Travelling overnight between Almaty and Tashkent in Uzbekistan, we were told to pull the wooden shutters down over our compartment windows. This particular sport was for local lads, riding on horseback beside the train, to shoot out lit carriage windows. No animosity intended, just good clean fun. It was a reminder of youthful exploits of my generation, standing up in the back of a speeding utility putting bullet holes in road signs. Nothing changes much. We were told that in a previous journey the train lost seven windows to the marksmen.

From then on there were no more threats from local rascals as the train made its way through several 'stans', rounded the northern end of the Caspian Sea and made its way into the Russian Federation. One thing about well-organised tours: nothing unexpected happens, and this time there was plenty of hot water in Russian hotels. The tour ended in Saint Petersburg where the city was preparing for a meeting of world leaders in the summer of 2003. Our hotel, the Nevsky Hotel Grand, was being prepared for President George Bush of the United States. As a result we had to walk from the nearest street corner along a freshly tarred road leading to the front door.

The hotel was originally built by the czars to entertain visiting heads of state. The first morning we were there, I went for breakfast in the grand dining room. A harpist was playing on the stage at the end of the room and food was served buffet style. As this was the first and possibly the last time I would have breakfast in such luxury I chose caviar and a glass of French champagne working on the theory one glass at eight o'clock in the morning would not hurt. I did not take into account the service. As my glass became empty, it was promptly filled by an observant waiter. It was a great start to the day. Rob, who chose to sleep in that morning, was slightly envious as I described breakfast in detail. The following evening we attended a special dinner organised to promote a Spanish winery for a cost equivalent to A$60 which included food, wine and entertainment. This was too good to turn down. It was also my sixty-seventh birthday. It was held in the magnificent dining room. Unfortunately for the promoters, the SARS flu epidemic was at its height and very few paying guests turned up. A good time was had by all, us two anyhow. It must have been good because when I woke up the next morning the serviette was still tucked into my trousers. As a publicity exercise I am not sure how successful it would have been as I can't remember the name of the Spanish company. But for us, it was an unforgettable way of ending our first Captain's Choice.

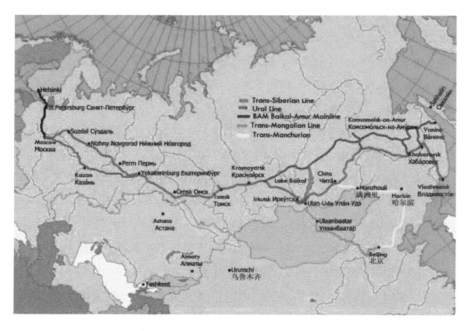

Map of the various Trans–Siberian train routes

We returned to Australia flying from Saint Petersburg to Heathrow in England and then transferring to a Qantas flight to Singapore where we planned a day's break. Arriving in Singapore we found one of our cases was stranded in England. Full praise to the staff at Changi Airport who tracked down the missing case and delivered it to our hotel the following afternoon.

TWENTY

Changes at Home and Abroad

The next year, 2004, we had a change of lifestyle, and a look at a new continent. Our home at East Hawthorn, Lothlorien, needed some major renovations. However, we had seen an advertisement for a retirement complex in Camberwell not far away. To us this was the answer we had been waiting for, so after due investigation and consultation we put a large amount of money as a deposit on a piece of air which eventually we hoped would become our new home. This was ready by May 2004.

After we had sold the East Hawthorn house and settled into retirement village life, we took our second Captain's Choice tour which introduced us to Central and South America. The company had hired a Qantas 747 extended range aeroplane along with crew to get us around the continent. Our first flight was a long one from Sydney to Merida on the north-west tip of Mexico and the centre of the long-gone Aztec empire. The Qantas plane was only the second Boeing 747 to land at the Merida airport which was actually 20 metres short of the required length for this type of plane. With the plane only half full and most of the fuel used up in the 16-hour flight from Sydney, the powers that be decided there would be no problem. The local television station filmed the arrival, whether because of the novelty of seeing the flying kangaroo arriving, or the chance we would end up running out of space, one can only speculate. We made it safely.

After admiring the feats and history of the Aztecs, our next destination was Havana in Cuba. The wonderful array of 1950s and early 1960s motor cars plying the streets captured our attention and cameras. This was all due to the embargoes on trade inflicted by the United States on the nation after their dictator mate, Batista, was overthrown by Fidel Castro's Communist Party. As no new cars were available the locals kept the ones they had going which gradually became a plus for the local tourist industry, an outcome not planned by the United States.

The flying kangaroo then took us into Brazil, first landing at Manus on the Amazon River. This is a port city some 2000 kilometres from the coast but it still surprised me to see large ocean-going cargo ships berthed at the city's wharves so far inland. The Amazon is a really big river. The next stop was Rio de Janeiro and with the beaches and the mountains it was exactly the picture I had carried in my mind. The visit included an interesting trip into the city's favela or slum area where the houses are literally built on steep hillsides, just about one on top of the other. In this area the rule of the authorities is only nominal. Our tour, in a convoy of four-wheel drive vehicles, was approved by the local criminal gangs which accepted our entry fee. This money, we were told, was used partly to provide education for local children and fill other gaps not provided by the government. There was also a local bus service going up impossible slopes and along narrow streets. It was certainly a rare insight into a way of life way beyond my experience.

Street in the favela, Rio de Janeiro, Brazil, October 2004

One of the features of the Captain's Choice tours is the opportunity to have half a day off in a town on your own and

Rio de Janeiro with the favela slums on the right, Brazil, October 2004

to poke around away from the tourist sights, although we were warned about some areas where it was inadvisable to go alone or in a small group. Travelling by air, regulations require that on take-off the usual safety demonstrations are carried out by the crew. These had to be done even on chartered flights. It didn't take long for the passengers to know the routine and patter by heart and eventually various passengers were invited to take over the role of the flight attendants and carry out the demonstrations following the recorded directions. Some passengers showed good acting abilities.

The tour took us to the magnificent Iguassu Falls in the south of Brazil and after due admiration we flew to Lima, the capital of Peru. Our destination in Peru was the ruins of Machu Picchu, high in the Andes. Our Qantas 747 landed in Lima and that was as far as it could go. To get to Cusco, the jumping-off point for Machu Picchu, we had to take two smaller planes provided by Air Peru that could land on the shorter airfield. From there the option was hiking or taking the train to Calientes Aquas, the small town at the foot of the mountain on which Machu Picchu was built. We took the train which zig-zagged up the side of one of the mountains and then found its way along a narrow gorge into the township. On the zig-zag at each switch of the points, a man physically changed the direction of the rails. It was another example of engineering overcoming immense difficulties.

There is only one road from Calientes Aquas to the historic ruins. It is steep, narrow and literally carved into the rock. Only buses with specially trained drivers are permitted to use this road as on one side is the cliff face and on the other side a sheer drop straight into the gully below. To make matters worse it was pouring rain, not unusual in this area. Our bus started the climb with the driver skilfully getting us around hairpin corners and passing returning buses with just centimetres to spare. It was a great display of driving under atrocious conditions. Rain continued to pour down as we carefully made our way around Macchu Picchu, being very careful of slippery rocks. It was an historic visit but I breathed a sigh of relief when our bus returned safely, in one piece, to the town. It was worth the trouble, the stress and the discomfort. This is what you can expect when visiting some of the wonders of the world. If you can't cope, my advice is stay at home.

Using a terrible pun, it was all downhill from then on. Air Peru got as back to the flying kangaroo sitting at Lima's airport. We flew back to Sydney with a stopover on Easter Island to view the famous statues. There was no trouble landing at the airport on the island. It was built by the United States as a southern hemisphere alternative landing strip for spacecraft. There was not too much accommodation for tourists and we were told our party had filled all available beds. Our short stay on the island ended with wonderful memories of a concert by a local choir and dancers.

The following year we got our collective breaths back by going no further than Merimbula in southern New South Wales in a more modern version of the Honda Accord. Age must be catching up with me because after turning 70, Rob and I settled for our second river cruise. Once again it was aboard the *Murray Princess*, the river boat we travelled on ten years before. Doing it the second time around there were no surprises. One could just sit back and watch the tall river banks go by and also learn more about the ecology of this great Australian river.

TWENTY-ONE

A Bite too Big

The following year, 2007, enthusiasm for travel overtook my ability to cope with the years that were passing at a great rate. I did bite off more than I could chew. It was a tour of northern Australia organised by a company called Outback Spirit. There was only a small group of people, 26 in all, travelling in a special bus with four-wheel drive designed for rough outback conditions. In some of the remote overnight stops we camped out in tents provided for the trip. It was managing my tent that I found was not an ideal way of travelling for a 71-year-old. The trip was well organised and some of the younger passengers did give the old bloke a hand with the tent. This did not stop me thoroughly enjoying the experience and because of the hard work I slept well on the stretcher inside the tent. The first major tour of the trip gave me another look at Kakadu National Park, including some parts I had not had a chance to visit.

From the Park our journey took us west to the Kimberley. I noted the improvement of some of the roads that I had travelled on twenty years before. I had always wanted to travel the full extent of the Gibb River Road from Wyndham to Derby and after traversing it on the Outback Spirit bus, I don't think it would have been a good idea to do it on my own. The main problem was that just out of Wyndham the road fords the Durack River. Water covers the crossing that is strewn with stones, which our coach had to carefully negotiate. The other problem was that, if stuck in the crossing, one faced the threat of saltwater crocodiles that also inhabited the river. Not a great idea. Further along the road near the Gibb River Station a heavy downpour had filled a cutting in the road with sand from a creek crossing. Our coach and its trailer could not initially manage the sand so to give it a firmer surface passengers pitched in to gather stones from the creek bed to provide a solid enough surface for our trip to continue.

Our tour was planned to take us from Broome across to the Bungle Bungles, the range on the eastern side of the Kimberley, and then from Halls Creek along the Tanami track to Alice Springs. Unfortunately nature intervened and during the night that we were camped out in the Bungle Bungles, unseasonal rain

Huts at Bellborn camp, Bungle Bungles, May 2007

poured down through the whole area. The following day it was still raining as we folded up soggy tents and packed the coach. The park managers then informed us the black soil road out of the park was impassable and we would have to stay another night. However, we were able to use the overnight accommodation at the tourist centre which also included meals, as the tour party booked for the night was unable to get in. Eventually the rain eased and the following morning we were told the track out was able to be used. In some sections, we passengers walked beside the coach to lighten its load as it cautiously drove through the mud. Eventually we reached the sealed Great Northern Highway.

The problems weren't over yet, as the heavy rain had made the Tanami track impassable. The only alternative was to add another 1500 kilometres to our journey and reach Alice Springs by the sealed roads through Kununurra across to Katherine and then along the Sturt Highway to Alice Springs. The coach courier (the

Our bus leaving Bungle Bungles, May 2007

driver's wife) and the driver took it in turn to drive and we safely arrived in Alice Springs still able to connect with our various flights back home. I decided that my days of camping out were well and truly over.

While I had been trying out one new travel experience Rob had organised another new experience for both of us. This was travel on the big cruise liner the *Sun Princess* and it was going to take us around Australia. This cruise started in Sydney so we used rail to get us there where we stayed with friends for a couple of days before joining a couple of thousand other people boarding the *Sun Princess*. We soon got the feel for big ship travelling. At the first evening meal at our assigned table, I apparently upset one of my dining companions by defending the ABC against what I considered some unfair and extreme criticisms. After the meal I observed the man involved and his entourage in deep conversation with the dining-room manager and never again did he or his companions grace our table. Comments from my fellow diners were along the lines of, 'Thank goodness he's gone.' You can't win them all.

The ship sailed serenely along the east coast stopping at various ports before turning left to berth in Darwin. On the way we veered into the Coral Sea to avoid a cyclone close to the Queensland coast. The ship had just come from a tour in North American waters and was still well provided with American and European beers. It appeared the company did not take into account the number of Australians on this particular tour and as we sailed through Torres Strait there were signs of a shortage of the Australian brew. Diplomatic relations were restored as a large semi-trailer, loaded with the Carlton and United brands, pulled up at the wharf in Darwin to restock the bars.

From there we curved along the west coast, stopping at interesting ports including a longer stop at Fremantle and then another left-hand turn took us into the Great Australian Bight. According to tales of sailors, the Bight was notorious for bad weather. I'm happy to say barely a ripple disturbed the tranquillity of the sea.

On the return trip to Sydney we called into Melbourne and we were rather tempted to take one of the sight-seeing trips provided but declined. Instead we introduced two American visitors to our trams. They wanted to travel into the city by this means so we got some tickets for them and put them on board at Port Melbourne. Yarra Trams was also aware of the tourist potential and were assisting people with tickets and directions as well as providing several special trams lined up for the visitors. It was well done. We opted for a lunch with Melbourne friends before returning to the ship for the final stage of the cruise which included a sail around Tasmania with calls to Hobart and Burnie

On the voyage Rob was doing his best to introduce the barman at our favourite watering hole to Australian slang including such phrases as 'dry as a dead dingo's donger' and 'how you're goin', mate?' The Chilean barman quickly caught on and surprised other drinkers with some of the phrases using a broad Australian twang with a Spanish accent.

TWENTY-TWO

From Sea to Land Cruising

By the middle of 2008 we had once again started looking at far horizons and thought, 'Why don't we go from sea to land cruising, going by train around Australia?' This is a bit difficult due to a shortage of railways. We had a heart-to-heart talk with our travel agent and it proved the point that the further you travel in a packaged tour, the cheaper it becomes per kilometre. The first stage was the XPT to Sydney. The cheese and ham croissants served by the train's buffet car are still to die for. Then we could just relax and watch the countryside go by. The next stage took us across Australia on board the Indian Pacific train. In the three nights travelling we soon got to know some of the staff and enjoyed the benefits of the lounge and dining cars. I find the pleasure in this form of travel is the time available to get to know well your fellow travellers who come from all around the world – much better than being strapped into an aluminium tube flying at a crazy rate through the atmosphere sitting beside someone who may or may not want to talk to you.

On this long journey, the first break is at Broken Hill where the train stops long enough to allow for a brief stroll around the city centre. At Cook we had our half-hour stop in the middle of the Nullarbor, allowing us to once again stretch our legs. We farewelled the Indian Pacific in Perth, and had a couple of days of doing nothing much before beginning the next stage. Due to the lack of a connecting rail link, we took a bus tour courtesy of Australian Pacific Tours which took three weeks to get us to Darwin. The bus was half-full, so there was plenty of room for all as we meandered north following the coast as far as Karratha, visiting many towns and historical sights and natural wonders on the way. No camping out on this tour, high quality accommodation all the way. From Karratha we turned inland and were shown the Pilbara mining area and the extent of this industry. On a remote road near Hammersley the coach stopped as a utility approached from the other direction. This was being driven by a friend of our driver. Apparently both knew they would be somewhere in the area at the same time and by coincidence they met. This was explained by the driver after returning from a chat with his friend.

During the trip if something unexpected or unusual turned up, the driver stopped and gave us a chance to see it or explain it. On the long stretches of travel between towns the driver played talking book tapes over the loud speaker, including the well-known tale of 'Red Dog' and we stopped at its statue near Karratha. I won't tell you the story, read the book; it's a great yarn. We continued our cruise through the Kimberley and at Kununurra I took the day off while Rob had a chance to visit the Bungle Bungles on a day tour by air. We had a launch trip from Kununurra along the Ord River to the huge Lake Argyle with its large amount of stored water. As well-organised tours proceed, we arrived on schedule in Darwin and were duly lodged in our selected hotel.

We had a couple of days in Darwin, which included the ferry trip across the harbour to Mandurah. Its main claim to fame is

'Red Dog' statue, Dampier, Western Australia, June 2008

the hotel. The old one disappeared during Cyclone Tracy in 1974 and is probably scattered across the Arafura Sea. The new one is well and truly anchored down with heavy steel beams and bolted-on roofing iron. One exhibit is a telephone pole twisted like a corkscrew, revealing the power of the cyclone. On schedule a bus picked us up from the hotel and took us the 20 kilometres from the city centre to the terminus of the Adelaide–Darwin railway to board the Ghan train. With the train about 20 carriages long, the bus drove along the platform to deliver passengers to the door of their compartment which was certainly appreciated in the tropical heat. Over the next three days and two nights we cruised to Adelaide on the train with long stops at Katherine, Tennant Creek and Alice Springs. An overnight stop in Adelaide took us to the last stage of the cruise; the daytime trip to Melbourne was on board the Overland train.

Another tour with Outback Spirit caught my attention, more so because no camping out was involved. This tour was to the far north of Australia, Cape York and the Torres Strait Islands. I couldn't resist this opportunity. Rob could, so I went off on

Hotel Mandorah, Darwin, June 2008

my own. The first part meant a flight from Melbourne to Cairns followed by a start the next day, again in the small 26-seater four-wheel drive bus but this time without the trailer and camping gear. As accommodation was limited north of Cairns many of our overnight stops were in lodges in national parks that sometimes were small stand-alone cabins. They were quite comfortable. In some areas one had to be aware of the menace of the cane toads and not accidentally stand on them as you stepped out. One of the stops north was the Lions Den Hotel at Helenvale and I managed to find my business card that I left on the wall on my first visit.

We weaved our way north going slightly west to see the mining developments at Weipa before heading towards Cape York. Briefly we travelled on the historic but now unused Telegraph Road which at one stage was the only route north, following the first telegraph line connecting the Torres Strait islands with the rest of the world. It was an important means of communication during World War II. Now a better development road runs alongside the old Telegraph Road, allowing conventional two-wheel drive cars to make the journey. The original road is now used by enthusiastic tourists and tour operators to give you a glance of the old way, complete with washaways, creek and river crossings.

A few years earlier, one of the biggest obstacles for travellers to the actual Cape was crossing the Jardine River. Four-wheel drive vehicles with snorkels could use the ford as the water was deep

Bus and sign at the junction of Telegraph and Peninsula Development Roads, September 2008

and treacherous. Rumour has it that in the 1960s some souls in a Volkswagen floated it across but I can't verify that one. The other danger is that the river is the home of saltwater crocodiles that have no respect for humans. Now a modern ferry operates around the clock. It travels about 100 metres from one bank to the other. While I was in the shop where the tickets are bought, one tourist was a bit startled to find that the cost was $80 for the trip but the return journey was free. Reflecting on the cost, it didn't surprise me as the nearest supply of diesel for the ferry was in Cairns, some 1500 kilometres away and the ferry operated every day. The ferry was also a source of employment for the local indigenous people.

We eventually made it to the top of Australia and, helped by the courier and the driver, this 72-year-old was able to stand on the very northern tip of the continent. The track from the car park to the exact spot requires traversing some very rocky outcrops

Jardine River ferry, September 2008

and I am well past the stage of skipping from one rock to the other like a goat. Nevertheless, I made it.

The remainder of the tour took us by launch to Thursday Island and this visit told me more about how close Australia was to being

Cliff aged 72 at Cape York, September 2008

invaded by the Japanese in World War II. There was the big anti-aircraft fort on Thursday Island and a visit to nearby Horn Island gave us the chance to see the wreckage of a Japanese fighter plane shot down as it attacked the airbase on the island. We were told two stories on the tour. Horn Island was the most heavily bombed part of Australia because it was the closest airbase to New Guinea. The other story was that the Japanese never bombed Thursday Island, believing that a number of Japanese pearl divers were on the island. In actual fact they had been removed as civilian prisoners of war at the outbreak of hostilities. It was an interesting lesson on Australian wartime history. The way home to Melbourne was without incident or much of a memory, as it was all by air from Horn Island to Cairns and then Cairns to Melbourne.

The following year we felt it was time for another cruise, this time by sea. The destination was Japan and it was aboard the liner *Dawn Princess*. The cruise started from Sydney so once again we boarded the XPT, and stayed with friends for a couple of days before joining the throng on one of the Sydney wharves. Enjoying a well-organised tour, we followed the schedules, and duly admired the tourist destinations as we travelled north along the west coast of the Pacific leaving Australia at Darwin. This time the cruise line had plenty of Australian beer on board. We called in at ports in Brunei, Malaysia, Hong Kong, China and Korea before reaching Japan. At each port a variety of tours were available giving passengers a chance to see the cities visited. They also gave the local 'businessmen and women' a chance to sell 'genuine' well-known brands of watches and pens at a fraction of the cost. There had been no change in the sales pitch since my first overseas trip fifty years earlier.

It was called the Cherry Blossom Cruise and happily the first of the cherry blossoms were in bloom when we reached our first Japanese city, Nagasaki. Here we were reminded of the devastation caused by the dropping of the first atomic bomb. Our next stop was Osaka. While we were on board a coach taking us to the tourist sights and shops, at one stop someone called out our names from the footpath. Two of our friends who also live in our retirement village were on a separate tour of Japan and noticed the coaches with the name of our ship *Dawn Princess* on a sign at the front and thought we might be on one, and we were. It was quite a coincidence in a city of a several million people.

Returning to Australia the ship travelled through some of the island chains in the western Pacific. These included Iwo Jima, made famous by the United States during World War II, the North Marianas, Guam, a United States territory, Micronesia and Papua New Guinea. Our port of call there was Rabaul on New Britain Island. There were still many signs of the recent eruptions of two volcanoes on each side of the town. These included banks of ash pushed from the roadways. The airfield also had some old Japanese aircraft left over from World War II. These were now buried under two or more metres of volcanic ash. The cause of a lot of the problem, Mount Turvurvur, was still rumbling and shooting out clouds of ash and smoke. At night, as we left the harbour, the fires inside the volcano were easier to see, and a little disconcerting to people not used to active volcanoes. We were able to calm our nerves in Brisbane before ending the cruise in Sydney and of course taking the train back to Melbourne.

My adventure for 2010 was another trip with Outback Spirit and once again they promised visits to some of the central Australian areas I had on my list to see but had not yet got to. Again, Rob declined to join me. Another friend of ours who I had known for many years, especially through our connection with amateur Australian Rules football, agreed to take up the challenge of visiting the outback. He was another Rob, Rob Acton who is now no longer with us. The tour started in Sydney but its first night out was in Wagga Wagga so we opted to meet the tour there, naturally taking the train to Wagga Wagga.

Once again we became familiar with the four-wheel drive bus with the 26 passengers and this time we were the two new boys as the other adventurers had started the journey in Sydney. All went well and on schedule as we eventually arrived in Broken Hill after stops at Mildura, and a visit to the Mungo National Park. As we travelled north to Bourke the news we were receiving wasn't good. The original plan was to travel west from Broken Hill to the 'corner country', Innamincka and then along the Strzelecki and Birdsville Tracks to Birdsville. Unseasonal rains had covered the centre, and combined with water from a summer cyclone in northern Queensland, had made the two tracks impassable. As a result we approached Birdsville from the east by way of Cunnamulla and Quilpie, staying overnight at Quilpie in shearers' quarters on Ray Station. They looked after their shearers well at Ray Station. As we approached Birdsville, signs of the big wet were evident as we carefully crossed several creeks with water flowing over the culverts. Any pictures of a dry and dusty outback town soon disappeared as we went past the waterlogged Birdsville Racecourse and the Diamantina River full to its banks.

We had a day in Birdsville and one of the options available was a day's flight to Lake Eyre and back. What was normally a view of sand dunes and dry saltpans had changed – there was water across to the horizon. All the saltpans, marked by dotted lines on maps of the inland, were full of water. The sand dunes rose from this inland sea. The lake is flat and a saltpan when dry. Our pilot told us that Lake Eyre was three-quarters full but it was hard to say when it would ever actually be filled. He explained that when the water comes down from the north it fills and just keeps extending as the lake has no defined banks. As more water comes down, the further it spreads across a flat countryside. Map makers put dotted lines to outline where the water might end up but these are estimates.

One of the amazing sights to see from the air were the flocks of water birds that apparently come from nowhere to Lake Eyre

Flooding around Birdsville with 'big red' dune, September 2008

Arial view of the Birdsville flood waters, September 2008

when it fills with water. These included pelicans, varieties of ducks and seagulls. Returning, we flew over the Birdsville track and it was obvious why it was out of action. The only way of travelling on it at the time was in a boat with an outboard motor. Our pilot took us over his parents' homestead, isolated by floodwaters near Innamincka, which we at least had a chance to see from the air.

Our plans to travel from Birdsville across the Simpson Desert to Alice Springs had also been washed out. Instead of turning west across the sand dunes at Boulia north of Birdsville we headed further north to Mont Isa, west to Tennant Creek and south along the all-weather Sturt Highway to Alice Springs. Incidentally for the record I returned to Melbourne by air. I went on the tour to visit the dry interior to places I had not visited. Instead I had a unique experience of seeing a flooded 'dry heart of Australia'.

TWENTY-THREE

From Road to Rail Again

In 2011 Great Southern Railways organised a train tour of mainly New South Wales. This time Rob was happy to take part in this train excursion. We didn't mind taking the Overland train to Adelaide where the tour began. Our tour train was named the Southern Spirit although we had a great time recognising the various cars

Southern Spirit train, Wauchope, February 2011

making up the train that had come from the Indian Pacific and Ghan trains. The tour was travelling in February which is off-peak for those two trains and obviously a good way of making use of the rolling stock. We didn't complain. We did sleep and eat on the train but for most of the trip the Southern Spirit did not travel at night so passengers could see the countryside.

During the day the train would stop for an hour or two and a coach excursion was arranged to take travellers to tourist sites. For example, on the first day we got off the train at Horsham on the way to Melbourne, had a coach take us to visit Halls Gap in the Grampians and meet the train at Ararat. We spent a night on a siding at Maroona just south of Ararat. From there the train, confined to the standard gauge, made Melbourne via Geelong and then used the only standard gauge northbound line to meet the New South Wales network at Albury. The tour then continued on to Wagga Wagga and stopped over night at Goobang, a small siding north of Forbes.

By now the Southern Spirit was using railway lines on which only goods trains operated. As a result our speed was limited as these lines weren't as well maintained as the ones used by faster passenger traffic. Still all we had to do was sit back in a comfortable lounge car and watch the countryside go by. It was not too hard a task.

Thankfully in the New South Wales network there are some cross-country lines remaining that connect lines radiating from Sydney to various points. This meant we could make our way from Dubbo east to Werris Creek and turn south to Muswellbrook. On the way we observed the real use of the railways in this area, the long coal trains bringing the coal from northern New South Wales for export through Newcastle. We did have a look at Newcastle by coach and then met up with the Southern Spirit at Telarah, a small suburban station in the city of Maitland. From there the Southern Spirit headed north to end the tour in Brisbane, but not before we had a coach trip to historic Port Macquarie.

We had a day off in Brisbane before returning to Melbourne and what better way to return than to take the XPT to Sydney, spend a couple of days in Sydney and then take the XPT in daylight to Melbourne. The ham and cheese croissants served on the train for breakfast were still magnificent. I rather hope that this idea of tourist train tours catches on. It's a great way of seeing the country and, with a demand for this type of travelling, governments may be less inclined to close branch lines and even reopen some of the more scenic routes.

Train travel was still on our mind later that year, 2011, when we received a beautifully coloured brochure from Captain's Choice enticing us to travel by train across northern India on board the Maharajas' Express. It was for 14 days in September, an ideal month to travel in India. The tour began with Thai International flying us from Melbourne to Mumbai via Bangkok. At Mumbai we had a day to spare before boarding the train. One of the tours offered that day was a visit to the Elephant Cave on nearby Elephant Island. To reach the cave entrance meant a long climb up steep steps. One of the options offered was being carried up by four local lads on a litter, obviously available for elderly and not too fit tourists. At the age of 75 I thought I qualified. The four men were certainly fit carrying 113 kilograms up the incline. Going up, as far as I was concerned, was quite interesting. I was worried about one young man on one side who was still being trained in the art of ferrying fat Australians up steep slopes. I did my tourist bit and the quartet was waiting for my downhill descent. I had been told not to pay them until you get back to the parking area. On the way down I was looking down a steep slope and thoughts were flashing through my mind of what would happen if one of my bearers slipped. It was definitely much worse going down than going up, for me anyhow. Having safely reached the good earth, I was quite relaxed in parting with more rupees than the scheduled agreed fee.

The next day we were introduced to the crowded turmoil of the big city of Mumbai. As we walked to the station to board the Maharajas' Express, the first lesson was on how to cross a busy street. The locals demonstrated to us that you just walk into the traffic and keep walking forward. The traffic is slow and the motorists will not run over you. Everything moves at walking pace, including cars, taxis and buses, not to mention the horse-, mule- and camel-drawn carts. There were also the men either pushing wheelbarrows or pulling loaded carts. It's an amazing mess that seems to work or at least move along.

Once on board the train we were shown to our cabins. Rob and I had been booked into one cabin. However, unknown to us, there was a court case over a dispute about the ownership of the train. Only two tour groups had been booked on this train and it was planned that some of the carriages not being used should be taken off the train. The judge presiding on the case wasn't having a bar of this. He didn't care where the train was; all he wanted was that it stay in one piece. As a result there was a surfeit of staff and carriages resulting in Rob having one cabin to himself, including a bathroom en suite, and I had the cabin next door to myself.

We were well cared for and of course well fed. We were also given the opportunity to try locally grown wine. My advice to Australian vintners? Don't panic. Settling in, we travelled

Peacock dining car on the Maharajas' Express, September 2011

across the subcontinent visiting the noted tourist destinations and marvelling at the extent of the Indian railway system with most lines now electrified. Only once did I see an overcrowded train with passengers sitting on the roof, and this was on a non-electrified branch line. At Jaipur I turned down the offer of a ride on an elephant up the steep slope to the Amber Fort. After hearing reports from passengers who used the elephants, it seems they were more comfortable than me in the back of a four-wheel drive Jeep that was the alternative transport for those unable or not prepared for the long, steep walk.

The Maharajas' Express dutifully wended its way to the Indian capital Delhi and then onto Agra for one of the highlights of the tour, the chance to see the magnificent Taj Mahal. Words can't describe it so I won't try. It is a good reason for making the effort to travel. At the holy city of Varanasi I was introduced to another very uncomfortable form of transport, the rickshaw, that took us from near the station to the banks of the Ganges River. I needed a bit of help getting into the seat, felt uncomfortable being hauled along by another human being, and the rickshaw was not well sprung or not sprung at all. As cows are a sacred animal in this area it did mean I avoided stepping into bovine excrement.

On the Ganges there were steps leading down to the water allowing people to bathe in what they regarded as a holy river. I admired the pilgrims' fervour as they bathed in the water on the presumption that their deity would cleanse them in what to me, as an atheist, was a rather polluted waterway. On the steps leading to the river a barber had also set up a stall to trim the beards of the adherents.

Our journey on the Maharajas' Express ended in the town of Siliguri on the eastern side of India, and south of our next tourist destination, Darjeeling in the highlands of the state of Assam. We

People on the banks of the Ganges, Varanasi, India September 2011

were originally going to travel to Darjeeling on board the narrow gauge Darjeeling Himalayan Railway train, otherwise known as the Toy Train. This remarkable railway, twisting and turning up the mountains to Darjeeling, was originally built by the British to bring tea down from the plantations and take visitors and English residents up to the cooler mountain resort. Unfortunately, an earthquake and heavy rain had temporarily closed the railway line. They had a Toy Train waiting to take us about 10 kilometres to the first landslide where a fleet of four-wheel drive vehicles was waiting to continue the remainder of the journey to Darjeeling, As we climbed up the mountain on the narrow road, we kept crossing the railway line, and in some of the villages the line just ran along the streets going very close to shop fronts and houses.

I was sorry I missed the opportunity to cover the whole journey, which would have taken six hours, but having sat in one of the carriages for possibly the first hour it would have been a

Maharajas' Express at Siliguri, September 2011

Toy Train passing land slip, on railway to Darjeeling, September 2011

rather stiff and sore traveller emerging at the end of the journey. While in Darjeeling I was able to travel to the other end of the line which was still operating. This train took us about another 10 kilometres to Ghum so I had a taste of the railway at that end. Reading the timetable at the Ghum station I was surprised at the number of trains which used the line each day. It was obviously a very important means of travel in this very hilly country in the shadow of the Himalayas.

During our stay we were told about the history of the tea industry and given a chance to see the plant being picked and prepared for sale. At the end of the visit, four-wheel drive vehicles took us to the nearest airport at Bagdora. On the way we stopped at Kurat, right on the border with Nepal. I was tempted to walk to the border post and ask one of the guards if I could walk across the line and stand in Nepal but decided against this. One becomes

Road to Darjeeling, September 2011

Toy Train at Ghum, September 2011

cautious in old age. An obviously overbooked local plane flew us to Kolkata where we had two days of sightseeing. Here we saw for the first time a tram service operating in India. It looked as though the trams were the original ones provided for the service. By their appearance they had been around for a long time. We avoided some of the tours offered and took a little time off to relax and get our breath back. Again Thai International returned us home via Bangkok.

Local tram at Kolkata, West Bengal, September 2011

TWENTY-FOUR

Over the Waves by Air

My former journalist colleagues, Tony and Elaine Wilson, with whom we stayed on the Gold Coast, had migrated to Vanuatu where they were working for a local newspaper and had happily settled there as full-time residents. After we had recovered from our trip across India we accepted their invitation the following year to drop in for a visit. This meant a flight to Sydney from Melbourne to connect with an Air Vanuatu plane, looking suspiciously like a Qantas plane with a different frock. This was not quite a smooth transition as our plane had been delayed in Melbourne and there was only a short gap before the Vanuatu take-off. Taking advantage of previous experience, we asked for airport assistance and were sprinted from one section of the airport to another on wheelchairs and made our flight on time. One advantage of old age. Unfortunately, I can't say the same about one of our cases which was still somewhere in the baggage handling area as our plane took off. Arriving at Port Vila airport I experienced that feeling familiar to most regular air travellers of watching the luggage conveyor come to a halt with no cases left on it, and no sign of the missing case. One advantage of your host being the editor of a local newspaper is that he knew who to contact. Eventually the missing piece of luggage was located still at Sydney airport. It duly arrived on the next flight the following morning.

This visit was our first introduction to Pacific Islands life. At that time of the year the weather was idyllic, but we were also shown the precautions that had to be taken to make buildings cyclone proof, similar to what we had seen in Darwin. There was also the lack of infrastructure that is taken for granted in Australia. Tony and Elaine had their own power generator and storage batteries housed in a separate shed which was their electricity supply. Like everywhere else there are pluses and minuses to living in an island paradise. Our hosts' house was on the main island of Vanuatu, Efate, and like many other islands in the South Pacific it had a mountainous interior. We were taken around the island on the road that follows the coast. Tony showed us the short distance of the road built by the Japanese. Its construction by the Japanese was abruptly halted when Vanuatu voted, along with Australia, to ban the killing of whales. After a delightful and leisurely fortnight, Air Vanuatu safely brought us back to Sydney along with all our luggage.

By now we had Honda Accord number three and this is where modern technology makes one hesitant in taking the vehicle off the beaten track. Twenty-five years ago I had no hesitation in taking my Toyota Corona to all parts of the outback, the same even earlier with the Renault 10, because I was confident I was able to carry out necessary repairs to limp the car back to the nearest mechanic. With many of the car's activities controlled by computerised systems they may be more reliable but if something goes wrong the traveller is stuck where the car has stopped. I could of course be getting old and grumpy.

The enthusiasm for travel was still with me at the age of 78 but I was learning that there were some factors one had to take into account. One is that the body physically finds it hard to keep up with the enthusiasm of the brain. A more telling reminder of one's advancing years is the difficulty of getting travel insurance as insurance companies, probably quite rightly, regard the chances of the person insured arriving back home in one piece as more of a risk when age is taken into account. With that mind, we decided that another train tour was on while the going was good.

The South African company, Rovos Rail, was offering a special once-a-year train trip from Dar es Salaam in Tanzania to Cape Town in South Africa over three weeks. Rob and I accepted the offer. Qatar Airlines was able to fly us to Doha in Qatar and then take us onto Dar es Salaam. On the advice of our travel agent we arranged to have disability assistance at each airport. For those who have got past the point of walking anything up to a kilometre between departure lounges at international airports, or are unable to stand in queues for anything up to an hour, it's an option I thoroughly recommend. This meant that wheelchairs or golf buggies got us from one point to another at the various airports. Our tour started off with a flight direct from Melbourne to Doha where we had an overnight and half-day break before taking our connecting flight to Dar es Salaam.

At Doha, we could see how the wealth from oil had transformed a desert oasis into a modern city of skyscrapers and magnificent buildings, but with no feeling of character. To me there was no taste of history to weave its magic on the visitor. We also learnt that although visas were not needed for Australian passport holders there was still an entry fee or airport tax for visitors of US$20.

Qatar is a strict Muslim country which bans the consumption and sale of alcohol except in the tourist hotels. These have very busy bars especially at the end of the working day as foreign workers along with tourists gather to mingle along with locals wearing European clothes. A sign at the entrance of the bars warns that persons wearing traditional dress will not be served and proof of identity may be demanded. The government-owned Qatar Airlines serves an excellent range of wines and spirits.

On arrival in Dar es Salaam we were met by Rovos Rail personnel and ushered to our hotel for an overnight stay before boarding our train. Our host was showing us around a small boutique hotel, as it was described, where we were to stay. In the main lounge the floor was covered with white tiles. Unfortunately, I didn't notice the step down into the central area and landed heavily on my shoulder. It was a Sunday and, while medical aid in the city is limited during the week, on Sunday it is non-existent. I was told that had my injury been severe the only option was a 1500 kilometre flight to Dubai in the United Arab Emirates. Luckily the injury was not so severe and I was able to continue the journey. Later, on my return to Melbourne, an x-ray revealed two small bones with breaks in them that had managed to heal on their own accord.

In the brochure we read that the train travelled at a maximum speed of 60 km/h so that travellers had time to enjoy the views of the surrounding countryside. Our guides on the tour pointed out that the sedate speed of the train was due to the fact that the British had built the railways about 100 years ago and there had been very little if any maintenance since. In the mountainous area of Zambia I watched from the lounge car window as the train of nineteen carriages in length carefully wound its way around the bends at about 10 km/h or even less at times. In this area we could see beside the railway line overturned goods trucks that had derailed as drivers had taken the bends too fast. I also noticed that two diesel engines were towing the train and directly behind the engines was a tanker full of fuel. It appeared that fuel and fresh water were occasionally hard to come by along the way. Despite that, in the en suite bathroom in our compartment there was a large bath, a relic of early rail travel, but thankfully there was also a shower stall. I did not try the bath as I wasn't sure if I could have got out of it without a lot of assistance.

As the train leisurely ambled south there were occasionally stops for sightseeing and coach trips which took us to such places

Rovis Rail train, South Africa, October 2013

as the Chisimba Falls in Zambia. As we approached the Zambian capital, Lusaka, we were told to pull the shutters down over our compartment windows. On the city's outskirts, a local pastime for young men was to arm themselves with stones and try to break the windows of the passing train from their vantage points on an embankment. One stone did land with a loud bang on the side of our compartment but missed the window. This reminded me of the horsemen of Kazakhstan.

There was an overnight stop at Victoria Falls in Zimbabwe where the local lads had made use of the country's hyperinflation by selling its inflated currency notes as souvenirs to tourists, asking for American dollars in return. After crossing the border into Botswana we left the train at Gabon and travelled by coach to the Madikwe Game Reserve in South Africa. Here we had a two-night stay and were given the opportunity to view wildlife up close and personal. Our park guides did tell us of the efforts being made to preserve the wildlife and did warn us that the animals were wild and should be treated as such. We explored the park in four-wheel drive open buses with canvas canopies and were told that the wildlife ignored these vehicles, but it would be a different matter if one ventured out of the vehicle alone. My faith in this observation was tested when a very large bull elephant meandered along with his herd of females quite close to, what felt to me like, a very small tin match-box. I did notice the guides carried a gun on the dashboard in the front of the vehicle.

At the lodge we were warned about the predatory monkeys in the area. Any open window was an invitation for them to enter the room and take any object lying around, particularly things that glittered. One of our party neglected to heed the warning and lost a small bag.

A coach took us from the game park to meet the train at Zeerust in South Africa, which then continued onto Pretoria. One stop included the Rovos Rail headquarters. A steam engine towed us a short journey into the company's railyards. We had a chance to stroll around and see some of the old carriages that had been recovered and were being restored for similar services such as the one we had enjoyed that the company runs in South Africa, Botswana and Namibia. Once the train was running on South African lines its speed increased as the state of the track improved.

For the first time in my life, and probably the last, I was able to have a close look at real wealth. We stopped at Kimberley, the centre of the South African diamond industry. After an

Steam engine at Rovos Rail headquarters, Pretoria, October 2013

introduction to its history and development we were ushered in through tight security to an inner sanctum. There on display were some of the world's largest and most valuable diamonds. They were indeed beautiful and with the security around them, out of my reach physically and financially.

One of the delights of the tour was dining on board the train. At dinner they served a four-course meal which sounds a lot particularly as one had been seated for most of the day. However, each course was small and accompanied by a glass of a South African wine to complement the food. A very good way of showing off the culinary gems of the country. This time Australian winemakers need to take notice of what is being grown on the other side of the Indian Ocean. We had opted and paid for an extension on our arrival in Cape Town that included two one-day tours, one around the coast including the Cape of Good Hope and the second one to visit the wine-growing area of Stellenbosch. On the first day, when the hotel desk told us our tour was waiting, we went outside expecting to see a busload of people waiting for us. Instead, there was our guide, who was also the driver, and a very comfortable car waiting for us. It appeared we were the only two to book the tour. As a result we had a leisurely tour of the coastal areas around Cape Town including the famous cape, and the next day the same gentleman was there to take us to lunch at a winery and a wine tasting, a very generous one too, and I was pleased we were being chauffeured around.

On the train tour we had met up with a couple from Cape Town who invited us to visit them on the third day of our stay. This is one of the joys of train travel: the sedate pace gives you a chance to meet and get to know interesting people. We had a delightful few hours at their home in one of the wealthier parts of the city. We noticed the contrast to the slums on the outskirts of Cape Town where thousands of refugees and migrants from other parts of Africa live. The South African government has been attempting to assist these people from more impoverished countries.

One of the features of Cape Town is Table Mountain, which broods over the city. Our hotel room window normally offered a very good view of the mountain but from the time we arrived it had been shrouded in mist or fog. On the final morning I woke up and was preparing to pack for departure. I yelled to Rob to get his camera; the fog and mist had cleared and Table Mountain was ablaze, lit by the morning sun, a magnificent end to a memorable stay.

Our first leg on the homeward journey was a South African Airlines flight from Cape Town to Johannesburg where our Qatar

Table Mountain from our hotel window Cape Town, October 2013

Airline plane would take us back to Melbourne via Doha. The airline won a fan for life because as we were waiting to take off 'sir' was offered a glass of French champagne which 'sir' accepted. There was a delay in taking off so 'sir' was offered a second glass of champagne. Any airline that offers me two glasses of French champagne before we have even taken off wins my favour. The return journey was a repeat of the outward journey. Doha hadn't changed, tall buildings and heat were still there. The remaining flight to Melbourne was happily comfortable and boring.

TWENTY-FIVE

Slowing Down

The following year was a quiet one. We limited ourselves to taking short trips in Honda the third as we settled into the routine of life in a retirement village. However, in 2015 I received a marvellous eightieth birthday present a year ahead of schedule. Rob booked us aboard a Qantas flight across parts of Antarctica in February. It was the only continent I had not yet visited. We had a slow start when a minor repair was needed, discovered when the plane was being carefully checked before takeoff. It was explained to us that once over the Antarctic, Christchurch in New Zealand is the nearest and indeed only place to land in an emergency, so everything had to be in perfect condition. We duly departed.

The flight consisted of four hours flying to Antarctica, four hours of flying over the continent and of course four hours for the return journey. We were also warned beforehand and in the air that, because of the unpredictability of Antarctic weather, changes might have to be made to plans at a moment's notice. On schedule we saw our first icebergs and then the mainland with flights over the French and Australian scientific bases and Mawson's hut standing out against the white background. The warning about the weather came true as we were heading for the Ross Ice Shelf. Flying inland over the ice, visibility dropped to zero as a white cloud enveloped the aircraft. Our pilot was forced to turn back over the same area we had previously seen but we saw it this time at a different angle.

As our flying height was limited to 1500 metres we did not see any wildlife. Suitable refreshments were served on the four-hour journey back to Melbourne. It was a trip that brought into perspective the vastness and challenge of this continent and a better understanding of the bravery of the early and even present-day explorers.

I celebrated my eightieth birthday on schedule on 29 April 2016 with a long lunch at my favourite restaurant. I decided my friends could all get together for a celebration while I was still around instead of waiting for the eventual wake which I wouldn't be able to attend! That's what eightieth birthdays are about, to my way of thinking. I also took the opportunity to launch my first book *My Life in Broadcasting*.

As I mentioned earlier, after the age of 80, travelling becomes limited unless you own an insurance company. With travel still in mind, what else can one do at that age but take a train journey from Normanton on the Gulf of Carpentaria to Melbourne. Admittedly, to do this you have to use a few buses as well. To get to Normanton we flew to Cairns, had a couple of days there in unseasonal wet conditions and then caught the scheduled Cairns to Normanton and Karumba bus service where we stayed right on the coast. A bus trip like this emphasises to passengers the vastness of Australia. After climbing over the Great Dividing Range from Cairns and travelling through the Atherton Tableland, for the remaining 700 kilometres there are no large towns to slow the bus down. The roads are sealed and in good condition so despite the distance the journey only took about ten hours.

Karumba is the main port for the prawn trawlers in the Gulf. Opposite the guesthouse we had been booked into was a local restaurant which served prawns that they had collected from the prawning fleet that morning. They were delicious and at $22 a kilo they were a bargain. Guess where we dined the following night? The next day, sated with prawns, the bus took us 50 kilometres to Normanton railway station to begin the first stage of our return journey on board the Gulflander. This train runs first to Croydon, an old mining town 145 kilometres south-east of Normanton. The line was built originally to take supplies to the miners at Croydon and bring back whatever they had grown or found. During the wet season the line can disappear under up to two metres of floodwaters. It was explained to us the track was laid in sets like a model train line so that the railway can be quickly brought back into action after the 'wet'. The top speed is a steady 40 kilometres an hour on this type of track. Although there is a lot of tourist

Gulflander train, Normanton, May 2016

traffic the train still acts as a commuter train stopping at small settlements and delivering mail and goods to some remote station mailboxes. The two-carriage diesel rail motor arrived vaguely on time at Croydon.

We were now on the organised section of our journey as a coach was waiting to take us to the start of our next rail journey, the Savannahlander from Forsyth to Cairns. Forsyth is about 150 kilometres east of Croydon and was the terminus of a railway that wound its way through mountainous country west of Cairns. This area was opened up by miners seeking gold and other minerals. The train served many communities that even now have limited access by road. It is now a tourist train, making one return trip a week from Cairns, taking two days to travel each way with an overnight stop at a tourist lodge at Mount Surprise. The coach, after picking us up at Croydon, took us to the Cobbold Gorge, a narrow water-filled ravine where the tourist boats only have centimetres to spare between the sides as they traverse the gorge. The next day the two-carriage diesel railmotor, passed on from some now defunct branch line, was waiting for us.

Again, this is a sedate way of seeing the country as the track winds its way through valleys and over ridges. Several times the train came to a halt and either the driver or the courier hopped out with a camera and photographed a flower or shrub. They explained that these photographs were passed onto James Cook University in Cairns. Much of the train line goes through country where there are no roads, hence the value of the photographs. At another time the train stopped, the driver got out, and came back holding a frill-necked lizard which he showed to the passengers. He said that quite often the lizard was in a certain tree and appeared not to be upset at all at being on show. This delightful informality made the trip interesting and relaxing. The overnight stay at the lodge at Mount Surprise was equally as comfortable helped by the hospitality of the locals.

The following day after crossing the Atherton Tableland we joined the Queensland Government rail network at Kuranda on the Great Dividing Range. There the Savannahlander waited to get clearance to make the steep descent alongside the Barren River to Cairns. Before each train descends, this section of the line is inspected in case there has been a rock fall across the track. We got the all-clear and our journey ended at the Cairns railway station.

Savannahlander train, Forsyth, May 2016

After a two-day stopover in Cairns, our rail voyage continued on board the new Spirit of Queensland train that has replaced the old Sunlander, which for decades connected Cairns to Townsville. The new Spirit of Queensland train takes 25 hours to cover the distance. The old Sunlander took up to four days although, since then, many of the stations it serviced have been closed. The sleeping berths have been replaced by aeroplane-style seats that slide out to full length for the overnight travellers. The same carriage has a bathroom with a shower and of course toilets.

On this stage of the journey we travelled from Cairns to Rockhampton arriving at one o'clock in the morning in a tropical downpour. The one taxi waiting at the station was able to take us to our hotel. We had alerted the hotel that we were going to arrive at this ungodly hour. The reason for the break in Rockhampton was to have a look at the changes that had taken place since I worked there 55 years ago. For this purpose we hired a car and a local driver to take us around the city and the coastal areas. This gave Rob and me a chance to see the differences without the hassle of traffic and watching where we were going.

Much of the city hadn't changed that much but the big advances were around the coastal areas. From Rockhampton we drove to Zilzie, now a thriving holiday resort. I remember it as a small settlement of several fishermen's shacks. From there went to nearby Emu Park where I had been a member of the surf lifesaving club. A new and much improved clubhouse had replaced the one I was familiar with. The hotel still retained some of its original structure but had been expanded and modernised, and it was still crowded. The day was a Sunday and it was legally open, which was not the case 55 year ago. At that time it was open for a drink in the late afternoon and I'll leave the legal aspect of that alone. Also, the big railyards where excursion trains from the mines at Mount Morgan terminated in the 1950s had disappeared along with the branch line itself from Rockhampton. Our driver then took us north along the coastline to the other seaside resort, Yeppoon, which has now grown into a very large town. From a lookout, I looked across to Double Head Point. When I was first in the area this was a bush-covered headland with not a building to be seen. It had since been developed as a marina filled with some fine yachts and of course houses all around. Progress marches on.

From Rockhampton to Brisbane we intended travelling on the Tilt Train, regarded as the fastest narrow gauge train in Australia. It is an electric driven train that can tilt up to 5° to go around corners thus saving time. Unfortunately, this chance was denied us due to track work so we had to settle for a quite comfortable long-distance bus which naturally was slightly slower but got us to Brisbane without incident. The remainder of the journey from Brisbane to Melbourne, which included a couple of days in Sydney, were on the reliable daylight XPT trains. Again, the breakfast croissants were up to scratch on the Sydney–Melbourne train.

TWENTY-SIX

My Final Yarn

Once you have obtained your OBE (over bloody eighty), as mentioned, your mind still has visions of ships, planes and trains taking you to strange places. Your body says, 'No, you've seen a lot and it is too difficult to climb steps, negotiate platforms and walkways and stand in queues, not to mention the kilometres between airport departure lounges, long wharves and the distances between platforms.' Then there is the trauma of learning how to operate the latest modern hotel room lights, air-conditioning and television set. As a result, I submitted to common sense and decided I would tell you a few yarns about travel. One final story though.

In 2017 Australia brought in laws allowing marriage between same-sex couples. After 47 years of living together, Rob and I got married at our home, the Prospect Hill Retirement Village in the Melbourne suburb of Camberwell, before a full house of fellow residents, friends and relatives on 26 February 2018. The honeymoon had to be another train tour. Again, it was the Overland train from Melbourne to Adelaide. Our first surprise was a small cake presented by the staff and Great Southern Railways

Marriage ceremony, Camberwell, 26 February 2018

to the honeymoon couple. I believe our travel agent had tipped off Great Southern Rail.

From Adelaide it was aboard the Ghan to Darwin. At dinner on the final night another cake for the honeymoon couple was greeted with surprise and pleasure by us and by applause from the other diners. From Darwin to Perth the railway line has yet to be built so for this leg we took to the air. For once the Qantas plane left and arrived at a respectable time. Both departure and arrival times were early and mid-afternoon due to the time difference between the Territory and Western Australia. We had a short stay in Perth that included a wonderful long lunch provided by a friend who lives in Fremantle. There are only hazy memories of this lunch due to the excellent Western Australian wines we sampled. Our tour continued on the Indian Pacific train to Sydney. We had the pleasure of once again meeting some of the staff who had looked after us on previous trips, making it a very pleasant and memorable journey. The cake for the honeymoon couple duly arrived during the final dinner aboard the train, again with applause from the other diners. I did notice one couple not applauding and looking very stern-faced. Friends met us in Sydney for a brief stay that included taking the train to Wollongong to visit a couple we had watched getting married some thirty years before. No cakes on the XPT from Sydney to Melbourne but the excellent croissants were still on the menu. Home for good? Possibly but I'm making no promises.

Ghan train at Alice Springs station, March 2018

Lastly

I have done a lot of travelling in my life. I have always had the desire to see what lies around the corner. At no time have I worried about planes falling out of the sky, ships sinking or trains running into each other. If you worry about that sort of thing, don't go outside your door and just be careful you don't trip over a mat inside your home.

Travel doesn't have to be expensive. My first trips were in the cheapest seats, in the depths of ships and at the back end of planes. Camping out, bed and breakfast places, cheap hotels with the bathroom and toilets at the end of the corridor, is a good way to start. As I earnt more money travelling conditions were upgraded

It's great to meet fellow travellers; say hello to the passenger next to you when you travel. Occasionally I have even found someone who enjoys a good conversation on planes. It's much easier on trains and ships – the travellers are not under as much pressure to get to their destination ahead of everyone else.

Another idea is to use public transport. Leave the car at home or better still sell it. Public transport will get you from A to B reliably, although not at the speed of sound and you can look out of the window without worrying about itinerant cars and pedestrians. I have used a day travel ticket to cover up to 40 kilometres around Melbourne on trips taking me to suburbs I had not yet visited for less than $5.

Finally, don't wait for the opportunity to arrive or to be dragged screaming out into the wild. Just get out and have a look while the going is good.

TRAVEL NOTES

Lightning Source UK Ltd.
Milton Keynes UK
UKHW050954190620
365163UK00002B/25